The Pilot Light

and the Gas House Gang

. . .The Life and Laughs of Frank Frisch and Other Colorful Baseball Characters

The Pilot Light and the Gas House Gang

by Bob Broeg

Introduction by Red Smith

The Bethany Press
St. Louis, Missouri

Cover photo courtesy of Brown & Bigelow,
and the National Baseball Hall of Fame

Design/Editing by Paula Hrbacek
Photos courtesy of *The St. Louis Post-Dispatch, The Sporting News* and the National Baseball Hall of Fame, Cooperstown, N.Y.
© 1980 by The Bethany Press

Library of Congress Cataloging in Publication Data

Broeg, Robert M.
The Pilot light and the gas house gang.

1. Frisch, Frank. 2. St. Louis. Baseball Club (National League) 3. Baseball managers—United States—Biography. I. Title. GV865.F7B76 796.357'092'4 [B] 79-27126 ISBN 0-8272-2927-5

Dedication

To lovely Lynne, who appreciated early that a writer must write.

Contents

Introduction

*(EDITOR'S NOTE: Walter Wellesley (Red) Smith, perhaps the most distinguished, literary sportswriter ever, has known Bob Broeg since "BB" was a World War II Marine. Red, columnist of the **New York Times,** knew Frank Frisch even longer. Smith barely was out of Notre Dame when he covered the pennant-winning Cardinals in 1930-31 for the old **St. Louis Star-Times** before turning his puckish talent to Philadelphia, then New York.)*

WHEN JOE McCarthy was manager of the New York Yankees, he would sooner put grenadine in his whiskey than speak well of the National League, its teams, umpires or individual players. In his mouth, the very name of the older league had low and foolish connotations.

One day he was approached by a reporter for the *New York Sun* who was polling baseball men on their notion of the ideal composite player—

a man who could hit like Babe Ruth, throw like Bob Meusel, run like Eddie Collins and compete with the fire of Ty Cobb. Joe misunderstood the question.

"What about Frank Frisch?" he asked. "What couldn't he do?"

From the day he came out of Fordham as a cross-handed switch hitter until his death 54 years later, Frisch never spent a minute in the American League.

When Frank was an elder statesman tending his garden in New Rochelle, New York, Sam Breadon, owner of the St. Louis Cardinals, spotted him across Toots Shor's restaurant in Manhattan. In the winter of 1926, Breadon had traded his great second baseman and manager, Rogers Hornsby, to the Giants for Frisch and Jimmy Ring, a pitcher. Hornsby is still regarded as the best of all righthanded hitters and that autumn he had led the Cardinals to their first pennant and a World Series victory over the Yankees. St. Louis fans stoned Breadon's car in the streets.

Now in Shor's, Breadon said:

"I'll be grateful to that man as long as I live. If he hadn't come through for me, I'd have had to leave St. Louis."

Sam may or may not have known about an incident in the 1931 World Series between the Cardinals and the formidable Philadelphia Athletics, two-time champions of the world with a lineup that could have marched into the Hall of Fame in a body. (Mickey Cochrane, Jimmy Foxx, Al Simmons, Lefty Grove, Eddie Collins, the coach at third base, and Connie Mack, owner and manager of that team, are enshrined in Cooperstown and others like George Earnshaw, Jimmy Dykes and Waite Hoyt probably should be.)

The teams split the first two games in St. Louis and moved to Philadelphia, where a Sunday rain forced postponement of the third game. Monday morning, Frisch climbed out of bed in the Benjamin Franklin Hotel, and fell on his face. Dragging himself to the telephone, he called Harrison J. Weaver, the team's osteopath.

"Lumbago," Doc Weaver said, and Frisch played the next five games strapped up like a mummy in Luxor. His record for the series: seven hits including two doubles, one stolen base, 42 fielding chances handled without error, five double plays.

In this book Bob Broeg tells about the longest home run ever struck—the one Frisch hit over and over as long as anyone was in earshot, all the way from Sportsman's Park in St. Louis to Back Bay Station in Boston. I remember it vividly, but even more vividly I remember another time when Frank did not hit a home run, or a triple, double or single. While he was struggling through a brute of a batting slump in that same season of 1931, the Cardinals wangled a narrow victory over a pitcher who allowed only three or four hits, at most. They were rejoicing noisily when I encountered Frank in the clubhouse.

"Well, Dutchman," I said tactfully, assuming that he would be as jubilant as the rest, "when are you going to hit one?"

My ears still twang like twin guitars when I remember his reply. Not the words but the vehemence; even under today's relaxed standards, the words cannot be repeated here. The breath whooshed out of me. I made my way back to the pressbox and told my boss, Sid Keener, about the colloquy. Sid howled with laughter. "That'll teach you," he said, "how to talk to a hitter when he's in a slump."

Two or three days later Frisch won a game with his bat. I did not seek him out but he saw me in the clubhouse.

"Hey," he said, friendly as a puppy, "I came out of my slump, eh?"

He was one of a kind. I'm glad Bob Broeg has written about him.

Red Smith

FRANK FRISCH
NEW YORK N.L. 1919 - 1926
ST. LOUIS N.L. 1927 - 1938
PITTSBURGH N.L. 1940 - 1946
JUMPED FROM COLLEGE TO THE MAJORS,
THE "FORDHAM FLASH" WAS AN OUTSTANDING
INFIELDER, BASE-RUNNER AND BATTER.
HAD A LIFETIME BATTING MARK OF .316.
HOLDS MANY RECORDS. PLAYED IN 50
WORLD SERIES GAMES. MANAGED ST. LOUIS
FROM 1933 THROUGH 1938 AND WON WORLD
SERIES IN 1934. MANAGED PITTSBURGH
FROM 1940 THROUGH 1946.

1

One for the Money Man

THE SHORT, stocky man squatting in the on-deck circle at Detroit's Navin Field raised his brown beagle eyes in surprise. The Tigers were going to pass the man at the plate to fill the bases for the Old Flash.

"Cripes." (Frank Frisch was more precise in his use of more colorful language of the dugout.) He could remember when the opposition tried to avoid getting him up there in a jam. Wasn't he the "money player," as the press put it? Another expression, "clutch hitter," gladdened his Germanic heart.

But as the 1934 World Series wound down to the moment of truth, Frisch had just turned age thirty-seven, a year older than the baseball record books showed. As player-manager of the St. Louis Cardinals' Gas House Gang, the veteran second baseman was tired. The Fordham Flash had become the Old Flash.

Frisch was once a blue-chip performer in the table-stake action of the World Series with the New York-based Giants, captain of three St.

Field Foremen: *Frank Frisch, 37, playing manager of the St. Louis Cardinals' Gas House Gang, poses with Mickey Cochrane, Detroit catcher, before the 1934 World Series. Both are in the Hall of Fame.*

Louis pennant-winning teams. But he hadn't hit much so far in the '34 Series. And maybe it was good strategy for Mickey Cochrane, the great catcher managing Detroit, to pass Jack Rothrock to get at Frisch.

Still, it hurt, and worse, what if Frank hurt his own ball club in that seventh-game showdown by hitting into a double play?

Detroit's pitching opponent of Dizzy Dean was athletic Elden Auker, who threw a confounding submarine delivery, dealing the ball from down under by dipping his right shoulder in an exaggerated sideward bend. The ball came up to the batter in a funny way.

The game was scoreless in the third inning. This could be the Gas House Gang's golden moment. But, if Frisch hit into a double play, the Tigers wouldn't have to get out his boy Joey (Joe Medwick) to retire the side. Even a guy as full of confidence as Dizzy Dean might be let down.

Dizzy, a rangy, rawboned kid of twenty-three, was making his third start of the Series after a spectacular season-closing stretch in which a

St. Louis surge, coupled with a New York fold-up, gave Frisch's fellows an unexpected pennant.

Dean, skinny, high-cheekboned flame-thrower, had started things with one out in the visitors' third. He "singled" to left. Dizzy had run hard to first, and then, acting as if he were a Pepper Martin or a younger Frisch, the St. Louis pitcher had kept on boldly to second, surprising Goose Goslin. With a hook slide the Old Flash himself couldn't have bettered, Dizzy had stretched the one-basehit into a double.

So when Martin, next up, hit a grounder, for which big Hank Greenberg at first base ranged to his right to backhand with his glove, Hankus-Pankus didn't have an easy forceout facing him at second base. Instead, he had to skid to a stop and throw the ball back quickly across his body to Auker, covering first base. And Pepper, running as hard as a scalded buffalo, just beat the throw on a bang-bang play.

Martin's infield single sent Dean scurrying to third, of course, and with Rothrock at bat, Pepper got a good lead and stole second. And now, with first base open, Cochrane had decided to fill 'em up by pitching carefully to the Redbird right fielder.

That put it up to the Dutchman, as most of the Cardinals called their manager, old number "3" with the white, red-striped, red-billed cap perched on top of his brown hair, as bald as a friar's in the back. They kidded that Frank's cap always came off because "how can you keep a round hat on a square head?"

Funny crack, but only at the right time. At this critical moment, there wasn't anything funny. Frisch stretched his old aching back by holding his bat behind his head with both hands as he got up out of that squatting position in the on-deck circle and slowly approached the plate.

Not only were nearly 41,000 crowded into the Detroit ball park, but high above in the pressbox, Frisch's friend, France Laux, was at the CBS radio microphone, telling a Depression-era audience about the pivotal moment. And, there were the Old Flash's good friends of the Fourth Estate from everywhere.

THEY'D all called him a great competitor, unquestionably a fiery-playing performer, but they didn't know that before the start of every World Series game—and he'd then played a record fifty contests in the national October spotlight—he'd wet his pants nervously. Sure, just like a little kid his first day at school. The Cardinals' equipment man, little Butch Yatkeman, kept the Old Flash's secret by keeping a dry jock strap ready.

But these pre-game yips had been different this time. The Old Flash, accustomed to eating heartily, had awakened nervously in his suite at Detroit's Booke-Cadillac Hotel. He told his wife, Ada, to order him breakfast: tomato juice, cereal, ham and eggs, toast and coffee.

Sick to his stomach, he drank only the tomato juice.

Now, as manager of the colorful, crazy Cardinals, pilot light of the wacky Gas House Gang, Frank Francis Frisch stepped into the batter's box. He glared down at florid-faced, raven-haired Mickey Cochrane, the Tigers' catcher, who glared back up at him.

Characteristically, Frisch polished the toe of his left baseball shoe on the back of his right stocking, then flicked the tip of the right shoe on the calf of his left leg. Next, grip slightly choked, he dangled his bat between his legs, well spread in a straightaway stance. Now, he worked the bat up and down, loose-wristed, in a preliminary exercise. At last, in an intense, overhanded chop, he began to wiggle-waggle the bat back and forth toward Auker.

The Detroit righthander was good, not great. He had been a brilliant all-round athlete at Kansas State University. He'd won the fourth game of the Series easily, whipping the Cardinals, 10-4, and he tried to wipe out of his mind the gamesmanship of Dean before the Series finale.

As Auker bent to whip the ball underhanded on the warm-up slab in front of the Detroit dugout, Dean passed, carrying his red jacket slung over his right shoulder and paused behind his pitching opponent. Auker glanced up when Cochrane, growling from the catcher's haunches, yelled:

"Get the hell out of here, Dean."

Dizzy, grinning, faced Auker and shrugging his shoulders, drawled:

"Hey, podnuh, you don't expect to get anybody out with THAT bleep, do you?"

But it wasn't a four-letter word that Auker fired at Frisch with the three-on, one-out situation in the third inning.

The duel was on. The count reached "3 and 2." Foul ball. Another delivery. Foul ball. Again, Auker whipped one from down under. Frisch just ticked it. Foul ball. The Old Flash rarely struck out, but now he took a deep breath, a sigh of relief. Another foul ball. Another and another and a seventh. Maybe they weren't all strikes because Frisch wasn't going to risk having that American League umpire, Harry Geisel, raise that right arm in a called third strike.

If they were close enough to swing at, they were good enough to hit. Auker grimly went through his shoulder-dipping delivery again and up came a sweeping curve. Frisch swung and the sound of contact, bat on ball, was sheer delight to the Old Flash's ears.

The gaffer started toward first base, those brown beagle eyes picking up the flight of the ball as it lined over High Henry Greenberg's glove at first base and into the right field corner.

When the white blur hit the grass in fair territory, Frisch went into his gallop. Once, that was one of the fastest movements in the game, but it was slowed now with the years. Why, in spring training, 1934, Branch Rickey, the general manager, had watched the skipper play second base at Bradenton, Florida and had confided to Gene Karst, the Cardinals' publicity director:

Turn-Around Talent: *The Old Flash, as Frank altered his "Fordham Flash" nickname, is shown as a switch-hitter batting from the left side at the moment of truth in the seventh game of the '34 series.*

"I ought to trade Frisch right now, to Boston for that catcher (Al Spohrer). Frisch is about through, but I know if I went to (Sam) Breadon, he wouldn't approve. Frank is still Sam's boy."

Sam's Frank was no longer a boy, with a spot of gray at the temples. He couldn't resist taking a gloating peek as he ran in the Series toward second. Long-legged Dean had scored. Wide-shouldered Martin had charged across the plate, too, and now Rothrock was past third, headed home safely. Three runs, the game and World Series were broken wide open. They floodgated to a seven-run inning and an 11-0 cakewalk for Dizzy and company.

Frisch, legs suddenly wobbly, stopped at second, and squatted there, happily, as coach Mike Gonzalez, his friend, and confidante as third-base traffic cop, applauded, silver teeth gleaming in a broad smile. In his cracked-ice English, Gonzalez chortled:

"You can do, Frohnk, You can do."

You bet. Frohnk could do, all right, and once again he had. The old money player had come through, but then so, also, had the many moods of a man who could be outraged or outrageous, a soft marshmallow or a tough nut.

Suddenly, it dawned on him. If he hadn't been so busy, watching his men tag all the bases, he would have been on third base, not second. To himself, Frankie Frisch, the Old Flash, snorted:

"Crissake, if one of my men had done that, I'd have fined him fifty bucks!"

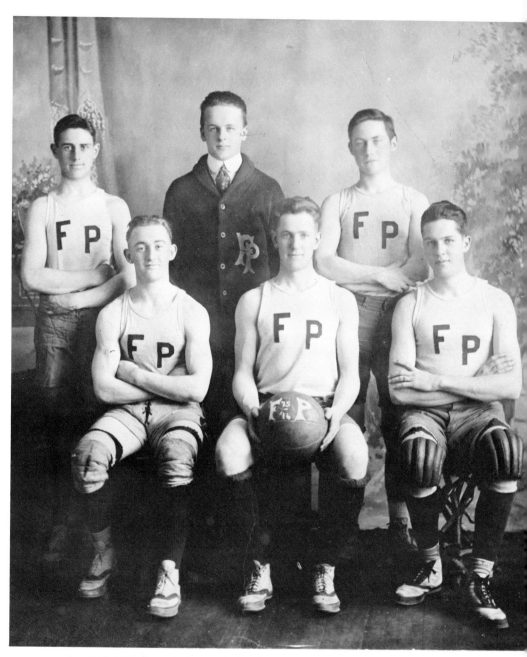

An "All-All" Man: *A baseball, football, basketball star at Fordham Prep and Fordham University, Frank Frisch, first row left, was a wide-eared prep school basketball star in 1916.*

2
The Bronx's Cheer

YOU CAN bet Mom Frisch's kalteraufschnitt, laid out in the family home for the kids in the Bedford Park section of the Bronx, that they didn't raise their second of four sons to play what Herr Franz Frisch reportedly called "feetball."

Herr Frisch was no Weber-and-Fields' character. Instead, he was a hard-working, intelligent immigrant who had risen from a $5-a-week clerk to a well-to-do linen merchant. Sure, he'd hoped the four sons would follow him into business, but he appreciated sports. Just as long as the brothers Frisch answered the whistle he blew at bedtime at the big clapboard house on Perry Street, Papa didn't mind. He wouldn't have to bounce a ground-rule double off any little Heinie's heine.

The old man really liked baseball and he took the boys to see his favorite, the bow-legged Flying Dutchman, Pittsburgh's legendary Honus Wagner.

Frankie Frisch—the diminutive as a nickname seemed to come and go throughout Frank Francis's life—played all sports with equal gusto. His father steered him gently toward baseball by sponsoring a ball club for which Frankie was batboy when he was just knee-high to one of Wagner's line drives.

Herr Frisch and a doting frau were afraid the son would get seriously hurt playing football, a sport at which he earned All-America second-team recognition when authoritative Walter Camp couldn't see much beyond the end of his nose or past Yale, Harvard, and Princeton. Even so, Frank suffered his worst injury playing baseball.

He played any position, a gutty little kid gifted with quick feet, hustle and heart. One day, catching, he took a hard foul tip squarely on the third finger of his right hand. Manfully, he tried to hide the broken, bandaged finger from Mama.

Trouble was, when the finger was treated, a piece of gauze stayed in the wound, causing an infection that, in turn, required surgery for removal of a piece of bone. So the ring finger of Frisch's throwing hand became as short as the little finger.

Ultimately, another baseball injury damaged another finger on the right hand, but fortunately, Frisch retained a good enough grip. It didn't lessen his strong throwing arm. Still, he didn't have adhesive hands, the kind needed for shortstop, the position he preferred.

So if Frisch, the magnificent all-round athlete, could be said to have had a weakness, it was that he lacked what the baseball profession calls "good hands." Cat-like quickness, a thick chest and moral fiber, the willingness to keep even a busted beak in front of the ball and both eyes on it, helped make Frank a topflight defensive player. These talents were combined with the ability to roam like a fourth outfielder for looping fly balls, the kind that were Texas Leaguers—except when Frisch would run slope-domed from under his cap to make a catch, often with back to the infield.

At Fordham University he captained the baseball, basketball and football teams. He was mercurial when basketball was more rudimentary and the bladder-inflated ball bigger. In football he was a stutterstep scatback who not only would break his share of long-gainers for the Rams, but, in the memories of the oldest observers, would display the backslapping, inspiration of a gungho leader.

As he would over the years in baseball, before the bench took away his ability to lead by example, Frisch practiced what he preached. For one big game on Rose Hill, home of the Rams when they weren't playing at the Polo Grounds, Frisch played with a taped broken hand.

By then, Frisch had quit using the nom-de-gridiron surname "Frank," designed to fool Papa. Herr Frisch was too smart to be hoodwinked by the coincidence of names and the red badges of courage his son displayed every Saturday after football. Franz certainly didn't get those scrapes and bruises riding with the horse-drawn sleigh Herr Frisch loved to glide around the Bronx.

Acrobatic Action: Frisch,
at Fordham, shows the
cat-like agility that attracted the New York Giants to
hire him off campus in
1919.

DESPITE strong Germanic ties, the family Frisch was glad that Frank
hadn't had to "go over there." Born September 9, 1897, the number two
son with those redundant first and middle names—Frank Francis—had
come along when William McKinley sat in the White House. So he was
spared by college enrollment and a heart murmur well before Woodrow
Wilson tried in 1917 to "make the world safe for Democracy."

Frisch, the manager, was subject to criticism after he no longer could lead his troops out of the trenches. But he was no dumbkopf in college even though, as he would suggest later, not wise enough to finish.

Years later, Bill Corum, the small-town Missouri boy who had become the AEF's youngest major in World War I and a polished sports columnist, asked a Fordham padre if he remembered a former student-athlete named Frank Frisch.

"Frisch," the priest searched his memory, obviously oblivious to the sports pages. "Ah yes, Frisch—excellent chemistry student."

However, after his junior year, Frisch's own body chemistry, as he neared his twenty-second birthday, would lead him to the Giants, then New York-based, for a $200 bonus and a $400-a-month contract.

At a time the reserve clause pinched ball players even tighter than high-button shoes, Frisch showed the kind of foresight that indicated he was what friend Mike Gonzalez would later refer to as "a smart dummy."

Even more than the Philadelphia Athletics' patriarch, Connie Mack, John McGraw was pitch-captain-and-bat-first of managers, doubling as an unofficial Giants' general manager for thirty years. Curiously, the powerful figure held still for an escape clause. If by the end of two years Frisch hadn't made good, the player would be given his unconditional release. Frisch could reassess his future and decide whether to go back to Fordham to finish his degree or perhaps learn the family's linen business.

Frankie Frisch was a rare bird, as well as, eventually, a rare Redbird. He never saw the day he put on a minor league monkey suit. Oddly, it was a game against one of the minors' best teams that convinced McGraw and the Giants that the kid they'd been hearing and reading about as all-prep this, and all-college that in New York, was more than just another promising youngster.

McGraw's old third baseman, Art Devlin, coaching Fordham, had been telling McGraw about Frisch. Then the Rams played an exhibition against the Baltimore Orioles, a powerful International League team·put together by Jack Dunn.

Against the professional Orioles, a story persisted that Frisch, the collegian, went "five for five." Wrong. "Only" four out of five, including two doubles and a triple, even though when batting right-handed as an early-day switcher, he hit crosshanded.

Try it some time: Righthanded, put your left hand atop your right and try to swing effectively. You've got to be good and strong—and maybe just a little bit crazy.

Under McGraw, the masterful martinet, Frank Frisch was a combination of all three.

3

Meet Mister McGraw

IF FRANK FRISCH had signed with a club other than the home-town Giants at a time the New York Nationals were the best, what would have been the young Flash's future?

Good question, obscure answer. It's unlikely that, born with a silver tooth in his mouth, he would talk as toughly as if he had teethed on a brass cuspidor. He could be polite, courteous, attentive and gallant among the opposite sex, many of whom found him cute even after his ample nose took a dogleg to the right from the impact of a bad-hopping ball. But Frisch could also swear like a salty Marine top sergeant.

Or like John Joseph McGraw, certainly the most influential man in the Flash's baseball life.

From the fiery field foreman for whom he played seven-plus seasons, Frisch learned many things. Other than a more colorful vocabulary, he also picked up some of the old man's disciplinary tricks, such as keeping a ball club sitting in the clubhouse until the moon came up, after they'd suffered a vexing defeat on a cabbage-head play.

A McGraw or even a Frisch wouldn't last long today, since the inmates took over the asylum, i.e., since ball players won extraordinary legal rights as well as the privilege to play out their options. The Flash and even Little Napoleon, as McGraw was described, would have to turn to sweet-talk or use a velvet glove. Else, they would wind up facing an arbitrator, judge or unemployment.

Like "Alice in Wonderland," Frisch learned many things from McGraw. He learned the smarts. That is, how to play the team game, a slick approach that included the now widely accepted strategy which never shows up in the boxscore—ability to hit behind the runner.

If first man singled or doubled, the next man up, the way McGraw drilled it into Frisch's head, HAD to try to go to right field. A basehit was a bonus, but mainly, the idea would be to make the second baseman field any ball, especially to that player's first-base side, negating a double play and moving up the runner. A basehit then could score a man from second or a fly ball fetch home the teammate if he had reached third with fewer than two out.

One of baseball's most durable managers, dapper Leo Durocher, a master manipulator as well as loud as a brass band, didn't credit many. But in his own book, *Nice Guys Finish Last*, the Lip acknowledged learning that lesson from Frisch.

Durocher said it gratefully and graciously, not grudgingly. And if you ever saw the Lip's teams play or those managed by his disciples—and he produced almost as many as McGraw—the team-game way of moving up runners by avoiding the double play was standard.

So the Lip got it from the Flash, but Frisch learned it from Muggsy, a nickname McGraw despised to the point where he'd fight. A previous Muggsy McGraw had been a sleazy, ward-heeling Baltimore politician when John McGraw played third base for the scientific roughnecks of the Gaslight '90s, the old Orioles. A short man with a short fuse, John J. simply wouldn't tolerate "Muggsy" any more than he would sloppy or unthinking play.

When a member of the Giants would say, apologetically, "I'm sorry, Mr. McGraw, but I thought . . . "

"With what?" Mac would snarl. "I'll do the thinking around here, you melonheaded so-and-so."

Or as he put it during the stretch in 1921 when the Giants overtook Pittsburgh with a pivotal five-game sweep, "We might win this yet if your muscles hold up—and my brains."

Conceited? Well, yes, if you want to say that he didn't think any two-legged son-of-a-sea-cook, or whatever he was calling them, knew more about baseball than he did. For most of McGraw's thirty years of running the Giants in New York, he was regarded as the smartest man in baseball—and the toughest.

Mr. McGraw and Friend: *John J. McGraw, grand tyrant of many championship ball clubs at New York, ends a 30-year reign by turning over the job to first-base star Bill Terry in 1932.*

Over the years, Little Napoleon became triple-chinned, double-bellied, and bulbous-nosed, with wavy hair that had turned a delightful white. He did indeed look much older than his years, but although he could be hard on players who abused themselves, he never seemed to forget a seamy boyhood.

As Irish as Hogan's goat, John Joseph McGraw was born in April, 1873, seven years after the National League was formed. Bearded boyhood idol U.S. Grant chomped cigars and sipped hard whiskey as President when Johnny McGraw grew up in Truxton, New York, close by Syracuse. He was a son of a section-gang worker who farmed a bit, too. Mac's mother died when he was twelve, and his father palmed off his four kids on relatives. Pop got Johnny a job selling candy on a railroad.

McGraw was a cocky candy butcher, bitten by the baseball bug at a time Cap Anson at Chicago and King Kelly of Boston were the big-name players. The little Mick on the railroads wanted to be a pitcher in the worst way, and cockily he'd argue baseball with adult passengers and customers.

By age fifteen, the 5-foot, 7-inch, 155-pound McGraw had settled at shortstop, then third base. He was sought as a fast lefthanded hitter. Although he had had other offers, and made other promises, he signed with Cedar Rapids, Iowa, for an impressive sum of $125.

Threatened law suits became old hat to the hot-headed Irishman, whose antics on and off the field brought him through the swinging doors of many a court room. But, as he said years later of his early problems, "I was just, really, a small-town boy a long way from home . . . ''

Indeed he was, but never naive. From the time he moved up to Baltimore in '91, the year before the Orioles advanced to the National League, the dark-eyed, good-looking eighteen-year-old was combative. His first day there, a large smart aleck sitting next to him on the bench nudged him off into the dirt. They had to pull McGraw off the startled playful character.

When Ned Hanlon came in as manager, the Orioles began to jell. With Wee Willie (Hit-'Em-Where-They-Ain't) Keeler and McGraw's two closest friends, catcher Wilbert Robinson and shortstop Hughie (Ee-Yah) Jennings, the Orioles combined foxiness with fierceness. They deliberately bunted foul so much, wearing down pitchers or ultimately wheedling walks, that the bunt-foul rule on third strike came in. And they made the one-man umpire as archaic as button-down uniform collars. That rascal McGraw, when the one man in blue was looking one way, would cut across from first to third by way of the pitcher's mound.

John had another little trick, too. When an opposing runner tagged up at third base, Mac would stand at the edge of the bag, facing the outfield, and as the runner poised sprinter's fashion to break for the plate after the catch, McGraw would hook his barehand fingers into the fellow's belt to detain him a precious step or two.

One day Mac got caught with a belt in his hands, if not egg on his face. A Louisville player, tagging up, loosened the strap. So McGraw was left, red-handed and red-faced, with the evidence as the runner scored.

But those were winning seasons for McGraw and his friends. He and jovial roommate Jennings showed something substantial, too, when they decided to go to college in the off-season. They were getting less than $1400 a season and couldn't afford full tuition, but they offered their services to teach baseball in exchange for courses on the St. Bonaventure campus at Olean, New York, where a grateful St. Bonnie established a McGraw-Jennings Field.

By THE turn of the century, a Cincinnati newspaperman named Ban Johnson was making waves with a new minor league, the Western. A year later he would opt for major league status as the American. Baltimore had run out of enthusiasm for too much success, but McGraw had not run out of ideas.

With the Orioles, he'd encouraged the bunt for basehits, not just sacrifices. Although the ball with which they played was a beanbag by comparison with the cork-center, then rubberized centerpieces that would follow in the first and second decades of the Twentieth Century, he urged the talented Keeler to hit-and-run with him. Mac could steal, but he could go farther and open holes in the defense for the wand-waving Keeler if he started in motion before Wee Willie pecked the ball through vacated infielder's positions.

With Baltimore folded in 1900, third baseman McGraw and catcher Robinson, the close friend, were sold to St. Louis for $15,000. McGraw demanded and got a fabulous salary at a time fifteen cents bought pork chops and a nickel big beer schooner came with a free lunch.

He was paid $9,500 for the season, insisting with a shrewd man's perspicacity that he be allowed free agency afterward. Mac could see a two-league salary war ahead.

So, dutifully, after hitting .337 for the Cardinals, McGraw emphatically fled St. Louis. As the train headed back east to Baltimore, where a new franchise in Johnson's new American League awaited him as manager, Johnny McGraw took his St. Louis uniform—and dumped it ceremoniously in the Mississippi River.

Anybody who knew the temperaments of Johnson and McGraw knew theirs was no baseball marriage made in heaven. Mac gave Ban and his umpires what-for so much in 1901, drawing the league founder's wrath in retort, that McGraw figuratively thumbed his nose at Johnson and the AL in '02. He jumped back into the National League as manager of the Giants.

They weren't kissing cousins thereafter, that's for sure. As Johnson stormed that McGraw had run out on Baltimore, Mac punctuated his profanity with a sage observation:

"I knew he (Johnson) was planning to move into New York, so I just beat him to it."

True. The Orioles were switched to New York as the Highlanders (Yankees) and Baltimore was without a big league ball club until the St. Louis Browns, as bad as the team McGraw took over in 1902, were bundled to Chesapeake Bay in 1954.

McGraw, finding the Giants groveling in the cellar, insisted on changes to owner Andrew Freedman, finally with a bellow that probably could be heard from Harlem to the Bronx.

Mac told Freedman in understandable, unprintable four-letter words what he'd do with some of the clubowner's bums if Freedman didn't. Then McGraw beckoned to Baltimore for a few stalwarts, including a battery that would break the bank today: pitcher Iron Man Joe McGinnity, and catcher Roger Bresnahan.

McGraw removed a big blond Viking from first base, a chap named Christy Mathewson, who had been consigned there from the pitcher's box the year before. Under the twenty-nine-year-old McGraw, Mathewson, then twenty-two, quickly became the game's greatest pitcher of the early century, perhaps the best ever. He was also the player closest to McGraw, the only one Mac wouldn't criticize.

Still, too smart to play favorites, McGraw would use reprobates if they'd help win, like eccentric, alcoholic Bugs Raymond, a pitcher he ran ultimately out of the Polo Grounds. Relieving, Bugs had slipped out of the bullpen onto Eighth Avenue and traded the new warmup ball for a couple of snifters.

If Mac liked a player personally, he would play cards or socialize now and then even though he had been married since 1902 to Mary Blanche Sindall, socially prominent daughter of a Baltimore contractor. With an $11,000 contract that would reach $40,000 plus bonuses, and profit-sharing, McGraw could forget active ball playing. He would play around, instead with horses he owned and a race track in Cuba. He was also a Broadway man-about-town who proved what many kiddingly say: That is, the Irish can't hold their booze.

McGraw's short fuse created many "scenes," including the time he used his fists on actor William Boyd. Boyd objected to vulgarity in front of charwomen at the Lamb's Club, where both were members. The fight with Boyd, not the silver-haired cowboy of the Hopalong Cassidy movies, got him suspended by the Lambs for three years. McGraw also acted like the politician Muggsy McGraw when he attacked umpire Bill (Lord) Byron, drawing a $500 fine and a sixteen-day suspension from the National League.

McGraw never tired of winning, never accepted defeat gracefully. From 1904, when capable John T. Brush succeeded Freedman as clubowner, until 1924, at which time Charley Stoneham and Francis X. McQuade had the team, and McGraw owned a piece himself, Muggsy won ten pennants and three world championships.

With virtually unlimited authority, McGraw paid well at a time when a dollar went as far as one of those big clouts by Babe Ruth.

The Yankees acquired Ruth from the Boston Red Sox in a spending spree reminiscent of George Steinbrenner's later. At the time, the Yankees were tenants in the Giants' new Polo Grounds, a horseshoe-shaped landmark at 155th Street. But hard-nosed McGraw told the Yanks they'd have to move. So brewer-sportsman Jacob Ruppert put up the first Yankee Stadium, aptly called by writer Fred Lieb "The House That Ruth Built."

It opened in 1923. By then some of McGraw's magic had been eroded by the livelier ball introduced three years earlier and by the down-at-the-knob batting grip popularized by the mighty Babe. Players no longer connived to a big inning or wheedled to a little one that meant so much, but just unbuttoned their vests as Ruth did. Scores came in home-run clusters.

If one got together old Giants who played for the club into the Depression Thirties, especially before McGraw lost his touch, a bloated sick man, one of them now and then might refer to him by his surname, although probably none called him "Mac." The reference usually is, respectfully, to the "Old Man" or even more to "Mr. McGraw."

They feared him, really, more than liked him. Or, more accurately, remembered his purple-necked, purple-prosed wrath and the fines he assessed—ten bucks here, fifty bucks there—more than they did the sawbuck or two they'd find in their locker if they'd come up with a game-winning hit, a game-saving play or just a smart move the Old Man didn't have to instigate himself.

To a man, they knew he could skin them, individually or collectively, with a tart tongue. As Frank Frisch would learn, first by observation and then as the victim, the man had a bad habit of using his captain as the whipping boy. Too often, as the seasons passed, captain Frisch found himself labeled the "dumb Dutchman" in front of the entire ball club when the Old Man was really mad at someone else.

John Joseph McGraw was—is—one of the most amazing, and dynamic forces in big league baseball's first century, past his personal centennial. But, long gone, he died when the Giants were up under another man and he was down, physically and mentally.

Maybe Mac had had it right, after all, when, trying to reclaim Bugs Raymond from Demon Rum, he had written late in his career that he felt "worrying over Raymond took five years off my life."

The diamond had known kings and queens as well as the Cohans and the Kellys, the Barrymores and the Bankheads, but McGraw had never known anyone quite like Raymonds. The Old Man blamed the press for use of the uncomplimentary nickname to which he believed the talented elbow-bender felt compelled to fulfill.

One day, fed up, McGraw held an opening meeting with the press and bleary-eyed Bugs. Mac read aloud a bill of particulars provided by a private detective who had shadowed the character the night before.

The gumshoe's report showed that Raymonds, who had promised to "reform," had sampled enough saloons to quaff forty-eight beers, almost a peck of pretzels and eight Bermuda onions.

At the end, Bugs was indignant. To the laughter of all, including McGraw himself, the poor soul with the wayward soles said, "That fella you had following me is lyin', Mac. I never ate no eight onions. I only ate three!"

Prime Time: *Frankie Frisch, the fresh kid from Fordham, dons the Giants' uniform he distinguished for years at second base, third base, at bat, and on the bases.*

4
The Series Sizzler

THE FIELD announcer bawled through a giant hand-carried mega-phone a lineup change for the visiting New York Giants at Chicago's Wrigley Field.

Witty Charley Dryden, Chicago's "Puck of the pressbox," couldn't quite get it and asked a New York writer seated nearby, "What did he say?"

"He said, 'Frisch batting . . . '" was the answer.

"Frisch? How do you spell it?"

"Frank Frisch—F-r-i-s-c-h."

"H'mm," said Dryden, dryly, "sounds like something frying."

Fizzling, not sizzling, would be more like it because that June 17 afternoon in 1919, fresh off the Fordham campus, Frankie Frisch went to bat for the first time in the big leagues.

31

Feebly, batting lefthanded, Frisch, who one day would be among the hardest to strike out, fanned on three pitches. He missed the last one, a curve, by an embarrassing foot.

McGraw, to whose club he had reported at Pittsburgh, a green kid wet behind the ears, called him aside.

"Young man, aren't you getting enough batting practice?" bellowed the boss to the speedster who couldn't steal first base.

"No, Mr. McGraw," was the polite answer.

"Well, see that you do," snapped the grand poobah of the Polo Grounds, who knew that, traditionally, regulars made it hard for yannigans, as scrubinis were known then, to get into the batting cage unless they came out early in the morning for three o'clock games.

Frisch was not known for asserting himself then. When he'd joined the club, he was awed by the handsome, high-ceilinged old Schenley Hotel, close by Pittsburgh's Forbes Field. Although it was known for excellent cuisine, Frisch frugally took his meals at a less expensive place down the street.

A few days later, the Giants' traveling secretary, Jim Tierney, scoldingly wondered why there had been no meal checks signed in the hotel dining room by the youthful Frisch. If McGraw thought the kid was out skipping meals to trip the light fantastic . . .

It was only then that Frank learned that all he had to do was sign for his food. The nominal daily limit was $3.50, but, Tierney said, Mr. McGraw didn't mind if an athlete went over the limit a bit, just so it was for solid nourishment, not liquid.

So it was that the rookie had to become more assertive, even in practice, rather than to stand around the infield. McGraw saw to it that the boy from the Bronx got to take his swings more often. With a fungo stick, the Old Man himself began to work him over. Result: Move over to second base, Frisch, you're no shortstop.

The Giants, who had been pennant winners two years earlier when they lost the World Series to the Chicago White Sox, were running second. Their second baseman, Larry Doyle, was the veteran captain, a former batting champion. Suddenly, jut-jawed shortstop Art Fletcher told Frisch to go to second base.

Frisch laughed. The league-leading Cincinnati Reds were in town for three straight doubleheaders, and . . .

"Don't laugh, busher," growled the veteran Fletcher. "The Old Man told me you're it. Doyle is hurt."

Frank gulped as fast as if he were stuffing down Mom Frisch's sauerbraten on the run to play with the kids back there in Bedford Park. Now, it was the Polo Grounds, the *real* thing. Before you knew it, the bell had rung. The Giants were in the field and Morrie Rath, the Red's speedy second baseman, slapped a hot ground smash toward Frisch.

If over the years Frankie Frisch had a buck for every ball he would knock down with chest or glove rather than field cleanly, he'd have been a millionaire. The first one was Rath's sharp bad-hopping ball that glanced off the college kid's muscular pectorals and bounded back toward the plate. Like a squinting cat hopping on a mouse or ball of yarn, Frisch leaped forward, grabbing the ball with that short-fingered right hand. He gunned the ball to first base, just nipping the batter.

On the Giants' bench, arms folded, McGraw nodded. One competitor had seen from another what he liked. Too many infielders would have flinched or would have panicked, either given up on the ball once they had kicked it or overpawed it.

Frisch would do.

Frankie hit pretty well in that Cincinnati series, but the Reds won the pennant, and the World Series when those heavily favored Chicago Americans highly talented and underpaid, turned out to include eight Black Sox.

Overall, leveling off, Frisch hit only .226 in fifty-four games, but McGraw had plans for him. Except to work him hard physically with the personal touch of a portly middle-aged man who recognized mechanical skills, McGraw paid him a supreme compliment Frankie didn't appreciate. He spared the college boy the mental ABCs of the game, the sharp side of the McGravian tongue.

To MAKE room for Frisch as a regular in 1920, McGraw shed the third baseman, Heinie Zimmerman, who had slipped as a former pennant-winning infielder. A fading Doyle was still at second base before taking his smile to Saranac Lake for years as a tubercular at a sanatorium. Yet Frisch had the ingredients for a great third baseman. He was fast coming in on a slow-hit ball, quick-moving laterally, and he had that strong arm to back up his fearlessness as a "chest" fielder.

The Flash was off and running. McGraw had broken him of that awkward crosshanded batting style from the right side of the plate. The press had felt certain Mac would compel the rapid-running ex-Ram to give up the switch-hitting notion as he had the Giants' aggressive right fielder, Ross (Pep) Youngs. McGraw had turned Youngs into strictly a lefthanded hitter, but he permitted Frisch to keep the turn-around technique, slightly corrected, that the Flash had first used at Fordham in a college game against a troublesome U.S. Naval Academy lefthander.

As a switcher, one who ranked probably with Mickey Mantle, Pete Rose or perhaps Garry Templeton, Frisch looked more natural left-handed. Like many turn-around batters, he was a low-ball hitter from the first base side and a high-ball batter righthanded. If it's said that he also knew what to do with a highball in either hand, that's no joke, son.

Righthanded, Frisch widened his leg spread to make himself shorter. Truly, nobody ever called him "little" even before he put on pounds with the years. The greater leg spread, righthanded, obviously was to make the ball at least seem higher. Actually, if not quite so impressive righthanded, the Flash hit the ball harder from the third-base side.

In 1920, the kid was playing extremely well. The Giants, rebuilding around the hometown boy, were doing quite nicely. Somehow, Franz Frisch Sr. managed to get to the Polo Grounds regularly, just as he had slipped into the stands often to watch Frank at Fordham. Herr Frisch had felt the second son was something special as a ball player, but now the sire knew it hadn't just been parental pride that made him believe that son Franz DID belong on the same field with the Flying Dutchman himself, the one and only Honus.

But then tragedy struck. The oldest Frisch boy, Charles, had died in his early twenties because of appendicitis, which was no minor menace before miracle drugs. And now Frank was stricken. The family Frisch was frightened. Even the Flash was scared.

Nine weeks later, more chipper after an appendectomy, Frisch finally was ready to play. He'd decided that—come what may—he'd rather take his chances trying to win ballgames than sell linen.

So, Frankie returned to the Giants and to third base. It was no surprise to McGraw that when the flashy lad from Fordham was back at the hot corner, hitting, fielding, stealing and talking it up, that the Giants perked up. Mac liked to think he could do it all with his own brain, but damned, though not quite so intelligent as McGraw himself, if Frisch didn't remind John nostalgically of himself.

Not that Frisch fought with his fists as often as McGraw had, but he didn't back down. Take the way he stood up to Burleigh Grimes, the stubblebearded, spitball pitching ace of the Brooklyn Dodgers.

Grimes didn't mind spinning the cap on any hitter, much less one who hit him as well as that fresh college kid. He began to bear down and in on Frisch fiercely, finding to his annoyance that Frank was an artful dodger if not a Brooklyn Dodger. And when Burleigh decided to go for Frisch's knees instead of his elusive head, Grimes was coming right down that lowball lefthanded hitter's alley. Frank creamed the square-jawed righthander's Sunday school pitch, a quick dipping spitter, the last LEGAL spitball permitted (1934).

Grimes, one of the best with the freak pitch, was a barrel-chested chap made more fierce-looking because he didn't shave before he pitched.

Against growling old Stubblebeard, Frisch showed moxie. He stood up there like a human pin cushion when he wasn't hitting Grimes' pitches. Naively, Frank would fling his bat to tangle up the feet of a bouncy young Brooklyn catcher, Zack Taylor.

"Hey," complained Taylor. "I don't call those damn pitches. You ought to know that Grimes pitches his own game."

So when Burleigh next sent the Flash sprawling in a tense battle between the rival boroughs' ball clubs, Frisch drag-bunted toward first base, hoping that he could get Grimes to cover so that he could bowl over the pitcher. Miscalculating, he came down with his spiked shoes on one of the Grimes' heels, almost severing the Achilles tendon.

When Grimes came off the injured list and next faced the Giants, he

G-r-r: *Boilin' Burleigh Grimes, square-jawed spitball ace, a Hall of Fame winner, was Frisch's early-day antagonist, and later his close companion.*

plunked Frisch painfully with a pitch, right in the middle of the back. Frank winced his way toward first, whining in that voice pitched sky-high when he was emotional.

"Dammit, Burleigh, I apologized . . ."

Sweetly, said Grimes, "Yes, but you didn't smile. So I didn't think you meant it."

If, however, Frisch had faced Grimes regularly, he doubtlessly would have done even better than his .280 in the first full season, driving in seventy-seven runs despite missing forty-four games.

He'd earned a raise, at any rate, and he got it. Doyle was gone: Laughing Larry, who once said, "It's great to be alive, young and a Giant." It was Frisch now who would learn the philosophical fun of doubleheader delight: personal success and pennants, too.

McGraw, who wheeled and dealt to win, acquired Dave (Beauty) Bancroft to play shortstop next to Frisch. Because Johnny Rawlings could play second base well, but not third nearly so well as the Flash, Frank stayed put in 1921.

The '21 Giants had a half-dozen .300-hitting regulars, including Bancroft, George Kelly at first base, Youngs and Emil (Irish) Meusel in the outfield and Frank (Pancho) Snyder and Earl (Oil) Smith behind the plate. A cunning breaking-ball lefty, Artie Nehf, headed a pitching staff that was just good enough. He won twenty games.

BY EARLY September, however, the Giants trailed Pittsburgh by
seven and a half games as the fun-loving Pirates came to town. Charley
Grimm, Rabbit Maranville, Cotton Tierney, Possum Whitted and George
Cutshaw were cutups. George Gibson managed the happy-go-lucky
Buccos. McGraw seethed.

"You're getting beat by clowns . . . clowns," Frisch remembered the
warm-up of McGraw's dressing down the day the showdown set began.
"You chowderheads, you dodos. Here I built this ball club, led you
around like puppies on a leash, and where are you? Well, I guess you
dadblasted, slab-footed bozos really don't even belong on the same field
with those clowns . . ."

The Pasha of the Polo Grounds, as free-wheeling free-lancer Jack
Sher called McGraw years later, was never better in that moment: a
Knute Rockne in flannels.

The Giants won the first game, but they trailed the second one by a
run in the eighth inning when George Kelly, the Giants' long-ball threat,
batted as Babe Adams, righthander against righthander, missed with
three straight curve balls.

. Hope for a tying base on balls? Wrong. McGraw flashed the "hit"
sign from the bench. A late-season New York acquisition, veteran
outfielder Casey Stengel, couldn't resist mouthing the surprise that ran
through the ranks.

"What!" Stengel exclaimed.

"Shut up!" McGraw snarled, seconds before Adams threw a fastball
with little on it for the so-called "automatic" strike. Kelly pounded it
high over the double-decked left field stands for a four-run homer.

McGraw turned to Stengel and said, icily, amid the backslapping on
the New York bench, "I knew Adams would lay it in there, and I know
what Kelly can do to a fast ball down the gut. I don't want only to win
this game: I want to crush those guys."

The Giants did for five straight games, the springboard to the pennant.
That's when McGraw sniffed and said that maybe if their muscles and
his brains held out, the club might win the pennant. It did, by two games
with a 94-59 record.

Playing the rival Yankees, who just had won their first pennant, was a
double challenge for McGraw because the Giants' tenants had taken the
play away from the National League landlords, largely because of the
one and only Babe. Ruth, increasing his own home-run record, had hit a
staggering fifty-nine, batting .378 and driving in a dazzling 170 runs.

By October, Frisch didn't know what town he was in, New York or
San Antonio, where the Giants trained. He'd come a long way from the
kid who had been so lonesome the previous spring at the Menger Hotel,
a New Yorker who was like Giants' fan George M. Cohan. He thought
everything outside Manhattan was Bridgeport.

Frank, actually born across the Brooklyn bridge at Ozone Park in
Queens, a borough of Long Island, had been taken to the Bronx when

he was a babe. So he'd grown there in the Bedford Park area near 206th Street, just five miles north of the Polo Grounds. Sure, he'd thrilled to those Giants' pennants, especially in 1911-12-13 and '17 when he was on campus because the Marines rejected him.

But now his heart beat faster, because a dream had come true. He was in a World Series with the Giants and against, of all teams, those rival Yankees. Frankie was so nervous that he swung "four for four" in the first World Series game in which he ever played.

Years later, grinning that rabbity grin of a pixie who opened his mouth to show only his upper teeth except when he belly-laughed, Frisch would say, merrily:

"I don't know whether I was numbly nervous or nervously numb, but I don't remember a blasted thing I saw or hit that day."

But he saw enough to rip all except one of the five hits given that 1921 Series opener by Carl Mays, who, like a latter-day Elden Auker, threw from the unusual submarine delivery, only more effectively. Mays, a 27-9 pitcher in '21, had a sparkling career won-and-lost percentage of .617 (205-127) for fifteen seasons. But he had a lousy disposition that cost him acclaim. So, too, of course, did the accident by which a pitch he threw in 1920 killed Cleveland's plate-crowding shortstop, Ray Chapman.

Mays shut out Phil Douglas 3-0. Top Series pitcher Waite Hoyt repeated the next day against Artie Nehf by the same score. The Giants hadn't scored and, worse, faced a two-game deficit no team previously had overcome in Series history to that point.

Moreover, the Yankees knocked out Fred Toney with a four-run third inning in the third game, but from the time the Giants responded with four against Bob Shawkey in the home half of the inning, the Series turned around like Frisch making a dazzling stop.

In the seventh inning, the Giants broke a 4-4 tie with an eight-run outburst, cakewalking to victory behind Jesse Barnes. And in the best-of-nine Series then played, the first in one ball park, and the first under Judge Landis's jurisdiction as scowling czar, McGraw's men surged past little Miller Huggins' big Yankees. The Babe had bowed out of the Series after the fifth game with an infected arm and wrenched knee. Only once in five hits had he reached the beckoning Polo Grounds right-field barrier, only 257 feet down the foul line.

McGraw was almost as happy stopping the "Big Monkey," as they referred to Ruth, as he was at the Series' sensational climax. In the eighth game, a result of an error, the only run (unearned) Hoyt allowed in three Series starts, Nehf led into the ninth inning, 1-0. Three outs to go.

After getting the Babe, pinch-batting, to ground out, Nehf yielded a basehit to the Yankees' second baseman, Aaron Ward. Next, the Giants' southpaw faced veteran lefthanded-hitting Frank (Home Run) Baker, the former Philadelphia Athletics' third baseman. Baker, still a threat at thirty-five, grounded a hot smash into the hole between first and second base, an apparent first-and-third single.

Rawlings, breaking to his left, flung himself to the ground, gloved it. From his knees, he threw to George Kelly at first base for the second out. Ward, rounding second in belief the ball had gone through, hurried to third. Kelly cut loose the arm that was so good that McGraw regularly had his lanky first baseman go out into short center field to serve as relay man on balls hit to the deepest part of the imposing funnel tunnel.

Now, Kelly's power throw zinged into Frisch's hands at third base. Ward slid high and hard into the Dutchman, sending Frankie sprawling backward toward the coach's box, but not before Frisch made a Series-ending tag.

Afterward, the Flash, flushed with victory and the prospect of a record winner's individual Series share, $5,265, just about a season's pay, urged back-slapping teammates to autograph the prized ball for him. Sweaty and keyed up, too many Giants wrote hurriedly and illegibly. The championship possession did not endure.

McGraw was so happy he threw a bootlegged blowout for his friends, the "swells," as they were known in the Roaring Twenties, meaning socialites, theatrical and sports luminaries. He entertained them with tales of how the Giants had done in the mighty Ruth and Company.

5

The Flash Flashes

JOHN MC GRAW had even more fun with Babe Ruth in the 1922 World Series. Frank Frisch enjoyed a spectacular series at bat. It was a year, too, when the Flash suffered an injury that would plague him past his playing career.

Constantly trying to improve, the Giants had tried to pry the slugging second baseman, Rogers Hornsby, from the rag-tag Redbirds of St. Louis. Hornsby had tattooed National League pitchers for a .397 average. Branch Rickey, Sam Breadon's business manager and field skipper, too, gulped and said no, but apprehensively. If Hornsby were hurt, the $300,000 offer would go a long way toward furthering the St. Louis franchise . . .

With a similar amount acquired from the sale of the Cardinals' old ball park in 1920 for a new high school, Rickey had already invested in his brightest brainchild—the home-grown farm system—by which poorer clubs could compete with the wealthier ones, especially New York, Chicago and Pittsburgh.

But Hornsby was still the franchise, the Cardinals' boxoffice answer to George Sisler, first baseman of the rival St. Louis Browns and a .400 hitter. So McGraw, who wanted the handsome dimpled Rajah as a gate attraction to oppose Babe Ruth, had to look elsewhere.

McGraw turned to Cincinnati. For $150,000 of Charley Stoneham's money and a couple of ball players, he acquired Heinie Groh, a great-hitting, good-fielding third baseman, thirty-two years old. Frisch would go back to second base and Rawlings to the bench as utility man.

That's the way it worked out, except, as mentioned, Frisch suffered an injury that would nag him throughout his career and beyond.

Down in Texas, the Flash was spiked in an exhibition game. The steel pierced his leather. It cut cleanly to the bone of the big toe. He limped off and moaned to McGraw, which Frisch could do eloquently. Although rough and ready, Uncle Frank had a bit of hypochondriac in him. Any genuine injury was dramatized.

Old Muggsy told him to go in, get the wound dressed, but to be in uniform the next day. "I want you working out, even if not playing, so that your arm stays in shape," he commanded.

Before Frisch could click his heels in deference to Der Fuhrer, McGraw had him back in the lineup. Until, that is, a stop at Nashville, where overnight the throbbing big toe pained and puffed. Even the managerial martinet could recognize an infection when he saw one.

Young Herr Frisch was forced into drydock. He missed twenty-two games. Thereafter, too, the Flash would wear a shoe a half-size larger on the right foot, although he had the dainty tootsies of a ballerina, exceptionally small for a stocky-legged man, even before his weight went up.

By now, at twenty-four, he had come of age as a hitter. Wigwagging his bat until it looked as if the pitcher would catch him with the wood pointed toward the mound when it should be cocked, he could slap (lefthanded) an outside pitch to left field. "Place-hitting," the trade put it. And, of course, from either side of the plate, he could go to right field. If you played for McGraw, you'd better be able to hit behind the runner.

Of course, that wasn't McGraw's only rule. He was known for his standards, his tongue and his fines. There are many "fine" stories, including the time a few of the guys got beered up in the hotel room shared by Frisch with the hustling right fielder, Ross Youngs. They began using light bulbs, water pitchers and other hotel possessions for target practice out the window. Then, when they heard McGraw and the hotel manager steaming toward the room, they scattered. Frisch and Youngs were left, in succession, with the mess, the bill—and McGraw's fine.

Boys would be boys, and the Old Man didn't mind if they indulged in a little good Prohibition beer, which was hard to get. But although he wanted his Giants to play rough and tough, they had to be gentlemen off the field. He elevated the status of the ball player, getting his ball club into the best hotels. Although still a front-office man with an eye on the counting house, he no longer infuriated the locals and yokels by parading to the ball park with a horse-drawn carriage which quite often displayed the sign:

"New York Giants—National League Champions."

The Giants of 1922 breezed to the pennant, a comfortable seven games ahead of second-place Cincinnati. They won easily even though Shufflin' Phil Douglas, a winning pitcher who bent the elbow too often, got himself kicked out of baseball with a stupid written "offer."

In a note undoubtedly written when crocked, Douglas, then 11 and 4, wrote Les Mann, St. Louis outfielder. At the time Branch Rickey's Cardinals, who would finish tied with Pittsburgh for third, were making noises like a contender. The Shuffler offered to "go fishing" if the Cardinals would make it worth his while.

Mann, recognizing a hot potato even when it wasn't cottage fried, showed the letter to Rickey, who sent it to Judge Landis. The commissioner ordered a hearing post haste. When Douglas mumbled that, yeah, he must have written it, he didn't get much chance to say that the signature should have been John Barleycorn. He was gone.

But McGraw had a good-hitting ball club, .304 for a team average, with six regulars or semi-regulars well over that mark, including a couple of outfielders for whom Mac had dealt the year before: Emil (Irish) Meusel and Casey Stengel.

Stengel, a jug-eared thirty-one-year-old veteran platooned in center field, worried about not having the legs to cover the deep part of the horseshoe-shaped Polo Grounds, which extended a whopping 483 feet down the middle. Cockily, Frisch, the young second baseman put him at ease. The Flash gave Casey that pink-cheeked Bugs Bunny grin and said, "I'll take care of you 'Pop.' Play deep, and the Flash will come back for the short ones."

Years later, Stengel's craggy features would light up, and he'd say, "And I have-ta tell ya that Mr. Frisch was correct. Out he'd come on the gallop, his cap flyin' off, and he'd catch balls Ol' Case couldn't have reached. Amazin'."

Because Frisch winced away that tender big toe and could turn his back and race toward the juxtaposition of the right field foul line and close fence, Youngs in right field could shade over to center field. That helped plug the gap for Stengel, too. Otherwise, balls would roll into the gap a subway ride's distance to those slanting-away stands.

The Frisch-Stengel relationship is worth exploring in more detail, but, for the moment, it's enough to say that the well-traveled Stengel hit .368 in seventy-seven games in 1922. And how often have you seen shortstops hit higher than Beauty Bancroft's .327 or catchers improve on Frank (Pancho) Snyder's .343?

The reliable Youngs hit a solid .331, four points higher than Frisch, who struck out only thirteen times and stole thirty-one bases.

Youngs, shockingly, would be dead of kidney failure within five years at only thirty-one, buried at San Antonio, where he trained for most of his nine-plus years with the Giants. Frisch, McGraw and others sorrowed over his loss. When Pep was elected to the national baseball Hall of Fame years later, Frisch, a member of Cooperstown's Veterans' Committee, was delighted.

How good was Youngs?

"Built like Enos Slaughter, and the same kind of all-out slashing player, but even better," said the Old Flash.

By the time the Giants played the Yankees again in the 1922 World Series, McGraw's busy brain had been both good and lucky. In mid-season, after Judge Landis dropkicked Douglas into obscurity, a sore-armed free agent, Jack Scott, at thirty, two years younger that Shufflin' Phil, wrote for a tryout. On a hunch, Mac gave it to him. Scott responded with eight victories in ten decisions.

The Yankees, meanwhile, proving they weren't a one-man ball club after all, had prevailed by a hoarse whisper over, of all teams, the St. Louis Browns. The Yanks had made the race the first thirty days without both Babe Ruth and strong-armed outfield compatriot, Bob Meusel, younger brother of the Giants' Irish Meusel.

Judge Landis, trying to curb a circus atmosphere that would dilute World Series interest, had directed that no players barnstorm until after the Series, then with no more than three members of the same ball club on any informal team. He forbade the Series participants to go at all.

"What's the old goat got to do with me?" roared Ruth. Accompanied by Meusel, best described as silent and sullen, he defied orders. The Babe found out that the old goat had a strong butt; thirty days' suspension without pay in '22.

Limited to 110 games, the Bambino fell back to .315, thirty-five home runs and ninety-nine RBIs. He became so distraught at one heckler that he climbed into the stands, clumping along the concrete on spiked shoes and chased the frightened customer, later identified as a railroad conductor, right out of the park and onto his choo-choo.

With the Babe over-eager to atone for an off-season and to make up for the physical—and losing—miseries of the 1921 Series, the Big Monkey was as ripe for the manipulating McGraw as the bananas the bench jockeys insisted the Big Monkey ate.

As Ruth pigeon-toed into the batter's box his first time, McGraw stood up on the Giants' bench and yelled to his pitcher, little lefthanded Artie Nehf, "Lay it over for him, Art. The big ox can't hit!"

The Babe backed out in amazement, then stepped back in, pounded the bat on the plate, and watched in embarrassment as Nehf floated a slow curve right over the middle. Strike one. McGraw gloated sarcastically:

They Ain't Smiling: John McGraw, who hated the Babe Ruth-led incursion into the Giants' championship domain, shows even less enthusiasm than the Babe for the formalities before the opener of the 1922 World Series at the Polo Grounds.

"Okay, Art, he didn't believe us. So tell him where you're going to throw the next one . . ."

Nehf nodded and told Ruth, "Same pitch." It was another soft curve, belt high, across the plate. The Babe swung, missed. Strike two. Heck, third strike was a formality. Ruth, hitting a miserable .118 with just two hits in seventeen tries and one RBI that Series, confided later that McGraw's taunts had tightened him up like catgut.

For the Giants, with the Babe muffled, the '22 Series was a breeze. They might have done in four games what took five, only because the second game was declared a ten-inning tie, 3-3. On National League umpire Bill Klem's bad advice that a long deadlock might catch the teams and officials in darkness, American League umpire George Hildebrand called the game. Uh-huh, when the sun still shone.

Judge Landis, a conspicuous front-row spectator, took considerable vocal displeasure of a crowd of 37,000. That evening the Judge erupted. He ordered all of the game's receipts, about $120,000, turned over to New York charities.

Even so, the New York Nationals humiliated the American League team. First, Nehf nipped Joe Bush, 3-2. After the tie game, Jack Scott, the castoff, completed his Cinderella season by shutting out the Yankees, 3-0, with Frisch driving in two runs. Hugh McQuillan topped Carl Mays in the fourth game, 4-3, and Nehf closed it out by beating Bush again, 5-3.

Although Groh had been a subpar hitter in the regular season, the third baseman with the odd stance, and even more unusual bat led all Series hitters with .474. Heinie faced the pitcher, bat held perpendicular in front of him in the equivalent of a military present-arms' stance. That bat, although naturally round under the rules, was rectangular almost down to the handle. They called it a bottle bat.

If Groh was great, so again in Series play was Frisch. The Flash, who had broken in with a four-hit game the year before, and then tailed off to finish with an even .300, came back strong in '22, creaming the Yankees for .471. He had eight hits in seventeen trips. And he toted off $4,545.71 as a Series winner's share.

Bottle Baby: Heine Groh, veteran Giants' third baseman and a hitting star in the 1922 Series, demonstrates his odd bottle-shaped bat and his military, present-arms' stance, by which he faced pitchers.

Frisch was a winner in more ways than one. By now, he'd impressed manager McGraw and ownership to the point he signed a contract for 1923, reportedly higher than the $12,500 said to have been the Giants' previous top, earned by the Old Man's former pitching prize, Christy Mathewson.

When Frisch signed his contract, the Flash said he planned to be married in spring training. McGraw objected. My boy, nothing could be worse for a ball player than a honeymoon, particularly when he was supposed to be getting ready to play ball.

Frisch gulped at the boss' lecture and broke the news to that girl down the street on Bedford Park's Perry Avenue, Ada Lucy, who remembered him first as that little German boy with the baseball cap. Ada was a quiet, soft-spoken woman, no beauty, but a Miss America inside. Although she could have no children, a circumstance both she and Frank regretted, she was a great helpmate, a homebody who gave the Dutchman a loose rein, yet could control him. And they simply adored and indulged her and his nephews and nieces.

Yes, dear Ada would wait until autumn to be married at her Catholic church in their neighborhood. By then her Frankie had brought her greater joy, if not the pleasure of another world championship.

In 1923, undoubtedly at his physical peak as he approached twenty-six, Frisch outstripped the entire National League in total bases. Yes, even the great Rogers Hornsby. The Most Valuable Player if there had been an award. Frank's league-leading 223 hits included thirty-two doubles, ten triples and a career high of twelve home runs. He stole twenty-nine bases and drove in 111 runs. The .348 average was the highest of his career.

So the sparkplug hitting on the number three cylinder in McGraw's batting order led New York home ahead of Cincinnati again, twelve points higher than roommate Ross Youngs. For the first time, briefly, the names of Bill Terry and Hack Wilson appeared in Giants' boxscores. And a name that would become prominent, Jimmy O'Connell, was there too.

For the eighth straight game, not counting that "darkness" deadlock the previous year, the Giants beat the Yankees in the opener of their third successive Subway Series. This opener was played at brand-new Yankee Stadium, the ball park Jake Ruppert had been forced to build by McGraw's attitude as landlord's imperious foreman.

It was Frisch, a .400 hitter in the '23 Series with ten hits, including a triple, who saved the first game for the Nationals, 5-4, with a spectacular play saluted in a newspaper commentary by Yankees' little manager, former second baseman Miller Huggins.

Hug's Series analysis came after the Yankees had risen like the Phoenix from the ashes of defeat to win in six games, gaining the first of the New York Americans' many world championships. And, by the way, Mr. Ruth gave McGraw a distasteful taste of what World Series crowds of the future could expect. The Babe blasted a double, triple and three home runs among seven hits, batting .368.

The Babe figured, however, in the play of the Series, as Huggins and others saw it. In the Series opener at the stadium, Frisch raced back into right field. There, Frank made a brilliant catch of Bob Meusel's looping bid for a basehit and then unfurled a strong, accurate peg to Pancho Snyder at the plate to double up Ruth.

Huggins wrote:

"The one great play of the Series was made by Frank Frisch. The

'A' Is for Ada: The girl first attracted to that "little German boy" down the block, Ada Lucy, married Frankie Frisch after the 1923 World Series.

play was the result of deliberation and quick thinking as well as skill in catching the ball . . .

"Frisch started for the ball with the crack of the bat, his back to the batter. Once he looked over his shoulder and saw that he had a gambler's chance of making the catch. In that flash of a second, he also started thinking about Ruth being on third. The crowd didn't think Frisch had a chance. We thought he had only a slim chance of a catch, not such a throw.

"Just the same, Frisch figured out a way of making the catch and throwing to the plate also. With the ball behind him and coming over his shoulder, he suddenly looked up and changed his course. By shifting, he took the ball over his left shoulder so that when he caught it, he could make a peg for the plate without having to turn all the way around. Now, if you will, bear in mind that he had to do all this while going at top speed and with only a split second in which to act; the speed of his brain can be realized.

"Frisch made a fast leap forward, caught the ball in his outstretched hand and without balancing himself, he whipped it straight as a string for the plate. It caught Ruth cleanly.

"Undoubtedly that was the greatest play of the Series and one of the most remarkable I have ever seen. If Frisch had been compelled to turn around to make the throw, the elapsed time would have lost him the play."

The game was won, actually, on thirty-two-year-old Casey Stengel's inside-the-park home run to distant left-center of the spacious Yankee Stadium in the ninth inning. Fact is, Stengel's seventh-inning home run off the original Sad Sam Jones gave Artie Nehf a 1-0 victory in the third game, the second and last one won by the Giants. Rounding the bases, Stengel, touching third, thumbed his nose derisively at the Yankees' bench. Someone wondered whether Judge Landis might take punitive action because of the unsportsmanslike gesture.

The Judge smiled and, proving he knew whereof he spoke, baseball's first commissioner said, "Forget it. That's Casey Stengel. He might do anything . . ."

Such as when the veteran outfielder, reduced by now to part-time duty, hit the game-winning blow just after Frisch had saved the game in the Series opener. Somehow, a result in part of a heel pad to protect a stone bruise, Casey thought he was running out of one shoe. He scuffled, accordingly, to keep from losing it completely.

The dramatic comedy of the race between man and ball was caught best by syndicated columnist Damon Runyon, who wrote at amusing length about Casey Stengel "running home his home run" in slow motion on tottering legs, chest heaving and . . .

Out in Glendale, Calif., the father of Edna Lawson, a tall chic woman scheduled to marry the baseball gaffer the next summer, shook his head.

"Do you think, dear," Mr. Lawson inquired, "that your Casey will last until your wedding?"

6

S-c-a-n-d-a-l

To COUNTERACT Babe Ruth's impact, which made John McGraw as green as the Old Man's Irish ancestry, Mac tried again to obtain Rogers Hornsby, by now hitting .400. The Giants would be glad to add a peacock's financial figures to St. Louis' drooping-tailed Redbirds. Players, too.

Branch Rickey, the master of circumspect, would be glad to talk. Yes, the Cardinals certainly could use the money to bolster the farm-system idea, which had begun to bear fruit, but, still, Hornsby was the best righthanded hitter ever.

"Would the Giants be willing to throw in a deal as partial compensation, their second baseman, that young fellow, Frisch?"

McGraw laughed. He wouldn't trade Frisch for Hornsby, even up, he was quoted in New York papers. What Mac wanted was BOTH men in his infield. He'd move Frisch back to third base and play Hornsby at second.

O-U-T: A victim of hijinks, 23-year-old Jimmy O'Connell was barred for life by commissioner K. M. Landis after acknowledging he had offered $500 to a rival player to "take it easy" on the Giants down the stretch in 1924.

But Frisch, why, he was almost as good as some writers suggested. As good now as—or even better than—the veteran Eddie Collins, the Columbia University whiz who had come up with the Philadelphia Athletics as early as 1907. Collins would play a quarter century on a half-dozen pennant winners for Connie Mack there and for Charley Comiskey with the Chicago White Sox. A .333 career hitter and .328 in Series play, he was a slick fielder, too, and a fast, heady base-stealer.

To Frisch, who always regarded Collins as number one at second base, the comparison WAS heady. But Frankie was almost as cocky as Cocky, Collins' nickname. Maybe the Flash was getting too fresh for McGraw, who, although he named Frisch captain with a $1,000 bonus when Dave Bancroft moved on to the Boston Braves as manager, found himself complimenting his star in a lefthanded literary way.

Sweetly, McGraw began in a by-lined column:

"Frank Frisch, the Giants' fiery and agile second baseman, came to me after our opening game in Boston and said, 'Mr. McGraw, I find there is something new to learn about baseball in every game I play. I wish I knew as much about the sport as you do. I would know it all then, I am sure. Will you teach me?'"

McGraw wrote he had been "dumbfounded" because "here was a youngster with so much natural mechanical ability as a player when I secured his services that for about the first time as manager I put a young player on the regular team without his having a bench education . . .

"Frisch took to it like a duck to water. His work in the field and at bat was phenomenal. In fact, his base running, too, was flashy to a degree. The college youngster jumped into high popularity with the Polo Grounds patrons.

"It was on this account and his natural ability that I refrained from coaching him, thinking it would be better not to hamper him with instructions that might handicap him in following up his promising start. I know by past experience that too much teaching of new things to young, green players has spoiled their usefulness, and put the brakes on their youthful ambition."

Here it came, McGraw's printed zinger:

"Frisch, by being given a free rein, developed an individuality that proved to be a detriment to the teamwork of my other players.

"To tell the plain truth, Frankie so desired to shine personally—that is, to win games by all his lonesome—that he became altogether too headstrong and took chances that were suicidal in their daring.

"Now Frisch did not, owing to his college enthusiasm, appreciate his fault. Sill, I hated to tell him, fearing to humiliate him. I wanted him to be cocky, to think he was as strong as they make 'em. I always did like that sort of player. I was one myself.

"This spring, after Frank, by a foolish attempt to score with none out, was nipped at the plate and after once or twice during our exhibition series with the White Sox, that wise old veteran, Eddie Collins, had rather 'showed up' my too daring Frisch by outguessing him on some play on the bases, I decided to act.

"So I had a heart-to-heart talk with my bold youngster and told him where and how he could improve. I advised him to get the fall-away slide—the hook, it's called—and taught him how. Before, he's slid into a base either feet or head first, but always straight on the baseline. Consequently, he left almost the whole of his person subject to touch. The hook slide leaves only a shoe or spike as a mark . . ."

Curiously, although Ty Cobb, Collins and other great early base-runners were adept at feinting one way and falling to the other side, the favored sliding technique for some time has been the direct approach. And this is what Frisch originally favored, whether belly-flopping or scooting in on the bottom of his baseball bloomers. The modern theory, whether using the pop-up slide employed by champion base-stealer Lou Brock, or just to get there with the "mostest the fustest," concludes that a straight line is still the shortest distance between two points. And although the bases are ninety feet apart, the instructional belief now is that a runner reduces the steps and distance to the next base with a good lead, walk-off start and straight-in slide.

Concluding his public airing of private linen, a business Frisch probably wished he'd been in when the Old Man's article appeared. McGraw wrote in an ending upbeat:

"I was greatly pleased, therefore, when the Fordham Flash came to me voluntarily for further advice. He had made a big hit by his flashy style of base-stealing, but he will make a bigger one later on. Frisch's improvement as a base stealer greatly enhances the Giants' chances for this season's pennant."

THE 1924 Giants, captained by Frisch, became the only National League club ever to win a fourth successive pennant, this time with a younger club. Groh was still at third base at thirty-four, but Frisch, just twenty-six, was an elder statesman. Travis Jackson, only twenty, played shortstop. An eighteen-year-old Freddie Lindstrom, became third baseman down the stretch. Bill Terry, twenty-five, moved in to play first base part-time, and Jim O'Connell, an engaging twenty-three-year-old kid from the West Coast, had become an outfielder as Stengel moved out.

O'Connell figured in a nightmare finish for the Giants. With New York battling Brooklyn—then called the Robins in tribute to rotund Wilbert Robinson—young Jimmy approached Philadelphia shortstop Heine Sand at the batting cage.

In light banter, O'Connell kidded about the pennant race, and wondered if Sand wouldn't just as soon see the Giants win as Brooklyn. Suddenly, the kid was offering the shortstop $500 to "take it easy" against New York, which barely led the Brooks.

Sand, startled, told O'Connell to get the hell away from him. Heine tried to forget, but he couldn't. He couldn't forget that Judge Landis had barred Buck Weaver from baseball only because the Black Sox third baseman in 1919 merely had known about, yet not participated in, the conspiracy to throw the World Series.

So Sand told the Phillies' manager. Art Fletcher called John Heydler, the National League president, who informed Judge Landis.

The commissioner ordered a hearing just about the time the Giants won the pennant by a game. Sure, O'Connell acknowledged having made the offer. Cozy Dolan, Giants' coach, told him to do it, the rookie said. Who else knew about it? Jimmy was pretty sure that Frisch, Youngs and George Kelly did.

The Judge called in the three players, guts of the pennant-winning ball club. To his satisfaction, they cleared themselves. As Frankie told his father, "Pop, I'm innocent, I swear. There's always a lot of kidding that goes on in baseball . . . "

But Dolan inferentially took the Fifth Amendment. To every question asked by the former federal jurist, Cozy had a cozy memory lapse. "I can't remember," he'd say, indicting himself.

Clark Griffith's Senators waited the Judge's pleasure in 1924 because, led by Stanley (Bucky) Harris, a sharp, tough, twenty-seven-year-old player-manager at second base, Washington had indeed done the unusual—won a pennant.

Landis, moving quickly, barred O'Connell and Dolan from organized professional ball, and against American League founder Ban Johnson's argument, the commissioner bade the Series begin. The Series was, appropriately, one of the weirdest ever.

Once again, Frisch was a Series standout. A .328 hitter in the regular season, he was trying to teach young Jackson at shortstop some of the tricks of the trade he'd learned from Fletcher and Bancroft. The Flash batted .333 in the seven-game Series. His ten hits included four doubles and a triple.

Afield, he was so sensational he won praise from his secondbase rival, Bucky Harris, the Senator's skipper. If it hadn't been for the Flash, Goose Goslin, the Washington left fielder, would have hit a ton rather than .344, which included a double, three homers and seven RBIs.

In the third game alone, Frisch made two brilliant stops on ground smashes hit by Goslin. More important, against the Goose in that game won by the Giants, 6-4, Frisch raced to the outfield, back to the plate, for a fantastic over-the-shoulder catch, just before Joe Judge walked and Ossie Bluege doubled.

"That catch saved the game," said McGraw afterward. "They don't make ball players any better than Frank Frisch. He's wonderful, always at his best in World Series games . . ."

Damon Runyon saw and wrote it this way:

"When you are old and feeble and the gray whiskers are hanging low, and you can't toddle out to the ball yard any more, but have to sit back and listen to the young folks gabbing about their great players—TELL 'EM ABOUT FRISCH.

"When they get to talking of the wonderful plays they see, about the slashing stops and the marvelous throws their players are making—TELL 'EM ABOUT FRISCH.

"When they start speaking of second base-ing in particular, and bragging of the way second base is played in their time—TELL 'EM ABOUT FRISCH.

"Tell 'em most especially about the way Frisch played second base, some of center field and a good slice of right field, too . . ."

Despite Frisch's heroics, the Series went down to seven games. Then Harris and his boss, Old Fox Griffith, outfoxed McGraw, whose Giants had been led by righthanded young Bill Terry, his platooned first basemen. Going into the last game, Terry had hammered six hits, including a double, a triple and home run, in just eleven trips to the plate.

How to finesse that handsome, dark-complexioned hulk of a man out of the lineup? Bucky and Griff had it. They'd start a righthander, Curly Ogden, to induce McGraw to use a lefthanded-hitting lineup. Then, after Ogden faced one batter, they'd bring in lefty George Mogridge. If McGraw followed form, Terry would be lifted. Versatile Kelly would move from center field to first base, Hack Wilson would shift from left to center and Irish Meusel would come into the game in left field.

The strategy worked. Ogden's warmup appearance did bring forth the Giants' lefthanded-hitting batting order. Harris permitted Curly to pitch to two batters, not just one. The teen-aged Lindstrom retired, but Frisch walked. So did Mogridge, in from the bullpen to face Youngs, who had led the 1924 Giants with a regular season .355.

Still, the ruse almost failed. Although Washington scored first off Virgil Barnes, the Giants scored three times in the sixth inning, one in which Meusel pinch-hit unsuccessfully for Terry, who had failed twice against the lefthanded Mogridge.

The late home-team deficit was rather sad. This was Washington's first pennant ever. President Calvin Coolidge, the stone-faced New England Yankee who didn't know a foul tip from a tip on that soaring stock market, was there with his delightful wife, Grace, who could keep a scorebook comparable to any baseball writer. And to top off the sad refrain, Walter Johnson, Washington's "Big Train" since 1907, had started and lost two games. This was the flame-thrower who would win 415 times for a ball club usually in the second division.

Suddenly, though, in the home half of the eighth at doll-sized Griffith Stadium, manager Harris hit a grounder that bad-hopped over Lindstrom's head at third base for two game-tying runs. And when the rejuvenated Washington crowd saw Johnson saunter in from the bullpen in the ninth, the roar was as great as if Congress suddenly had repealed the Volstead Act.

It was Sir Walter—Johnson himself, the polite, sidewheeling fireballer. But Washington hearts sank when Frisch, that clutch-hitting so-and-so, pickled the Big Train's first pitch for a triple. Here, the thirty-six-year-old artist who had only two pitches—a fast ball and one that was even faster—struck out Youngs and Kelly, then retired Meusel to make the disastrous start a scoreless inning.,

Two innings later, Frisch came up with a man on third. Frisch, the money player, the guy who seldom struck out, fanned. Years later, he would remember, "The old buzzard must have had a pea-shooter. I'm glad I didn't hit against him in his prime."

In Washington's twelfth, light-hitting catcher, Muddy Ruel, lifted one of reliever Jack Bentley's pitches for a one-out foul to rival receiver Hank Gowdy. Old Goldenrod Gowdy, a hero of the "miracle" Boston Braves' 1914 World Series, pounded his fist, stepped to catch the ball and tripped over his own mask.

Ruel, reprieved, doubled. Johnson, next up, grounded to Jackson, who fumbled as Ruel held second. Then Washington's leadoff man, Earl McNeely, hit a sharp grounder to Lindstrom at third.

On the Giants' bench, Billy Southworth, a reserve New York outfielder best known for managing four pennant-winning teams later, reached for his glove.

"By then," he explained, "I knew the gremlins were against us." McNeely's ball hit a pebble or clod of dirt. It hopped high over Lindstrom's head. Ruel, rounding third, romped home with the run that gave Walter Johnson and Washington a 4-3 victory and a world championship. It was the last World Series for John McGraw, and the last Frank Frisch would know as a member of his beloved Giants.

On the train ride back to New York, losing pitcher Jack Bentley said, philosophically:

"I guess the good Lord just couldn't stand to see Walter Johnson lose another one!"

7
Disaster, Desertion, Deal

FOR MONEY player Frank Frisch, the annual World Series share had become the equivalent of a yearly bonus, something to seek and to be invested. Even those losing shares of $4,112.88 in 1923 and $3,820.29 in '24 weren't bad, not for the perennial pennant-winners' captain whose club-record salary was about $17,500.

It was the jazz age, the time of the raccoon coat, the hip flask. The Roaring Twenties were good. The stock market, like women's dresses, kept going up. And politicians were talking about two cars in every garage and to heck with a chicken in every pot. Make it a couple of chesty capons.

Florida, discovered in a search for the fountain of youth, had suddenly produced the gold that earlier sent Spanish explorer Cortez into Mexico's halls of Montezuma. The difference was that the Sunshine

State's gold was its real estate, dirt cheap and sky high, if you believed the promoters.

They were swamped with buyers for what often was swampland. The Giants had moved from Texas to Sarasota because that show-biz caterer to the prominent, John McGraw, had become bosom buddies with the Ringlings, the circus people who wintered in Sarasota.

There, the fat-cat Giants joined in the get-rich-quick schemes of real-estate developments, partly out of greed and partly because the Old Man himself had set up his own planned settlement in a salubrious section called "Pennant Park." The ball players went in, a little or a lot. Among them was captain Frisch.

The Dutchman was a paradox throughout his life. He'd spend lavishly for creature comforts, partly as a gourmet who bordered on the gourmand, but he could beef, if you'll pardon the pun, about the price of a set of tires. Although known to clubhouse boys, waiters and others who serviced him as a generous tipper, some observers thought he was tight with a buck.

Those dollars had come hard, all right. So it was a double jolt to the Flash. Although he had another typical Frischian season in 1925, hitting .331 even though moved from second base to third and even shortstop at times as now the oldest man, twenty-seven, the Giants finished a poor second to Bill McKechnie's Pittsburgh Pirates. The pitching was subpar. Not even McGraw, characteristically calling all the pitches from the bench, could make chicken salad out of chicken feathers.

So there would be no Series check for Frisch to invest or to spend while enjoying the winter with Ada. Even worse, the real estate boom in Florida collapsed sickeningly, most certainly in Sarasota. Grimly, McGraw paid off persons who had invested directly through him.

Frisch, bemoaning his losses, held out in the spring of 1926, reporting late. McGraw, adamant, noted that the club had set salaries. For three years the captain already had been the highest-paid player on the ball club.

So the atmosphere wasn't good in 1926, a year to remember. A dumpy New York girl named Gertrude Ederle swam the English channel. Dashing, dapper-mustached Douglas Fairbanks, Sr. made the first part-color movie, a swashbuckler called *The Black Pirate*. St. Louis Cardinals claimed on $4,500 waivers at mid-June a famous old pitcher whose drinking habits finally had worn thin on manager Joe McCarthy at Chicago.

Grover Cleveland Alexander, nearing forty, would become the baseball story of the year, but not before Frisch made news in August. As always, McGraw had used the captain as his whipping boy. The carping had eroded Frisch. The Flash sniffled with a summer cold in a game against the Cardinals at old Sportsman's Park. McGraw flashed a sign.

With Cardinals on first and third, Mac suspected a double steal, but he didn't want the catcher to throw through. He wanted the ball pegged back to the pitcher, hoping to trap the runner off third, unconcerned whether the man on first reached second. So there was no need for either the second baseman or shortstop to cover. But, although Frisch did not acknowledge missing the sign, when the runner on first broke for second, Frankie moved to his right to cover the base.

St. Louis' light-hitting shortstop, righthanded-batting Tommy Thevenow, poked at the pitch and dribbled a slow grounder to Frisch's left. The Flash put on the brakes, but he couldn't get back. The ball went through for a decisive base hit.

Afterward, McGraw's attack on Frisch was frontal. "You dumb Dutchman," he warmed up, "you cement head . . . "

Frisch hated to lose as much as McGraw did. He was sore in spirit and body. He took what amounted to extra innings of castigation, his cup of bitterness overflowing. Afterward, ears burning, he went out with Irish Meusel and Long George Kelly.

Kelly and Youngs offered not tea and sympathy, but a couple of speakeasy bottles of home brew. Then Frisch returned to the Buckingham Hotel. He couldn't sleep. Finally, he came to a decision. Frank called a bellman to his room, tipped him five dollars and asked him to make a reservation on the noon train to New York, then arrange to pick up Frisch's bags in the A.M. while the Flash breakfasted.

The next morning, a cub baseball reporter for a New York newspaper, feeding the pigeons outside the hotel, missed one helluva story. He saw the Giants' captain, Frank Frisch, get into a taxicab with his bags. Slow-witted, the young writer didn't add two and two.

When Frisch settled into the train's parlor car to read, trying to quiet nerves strained by the boldness of his decision, a man eyed him intently.

"Aren't you playing today?" the man asked.

The tanned athlete pretended not to understand.

"Aren't you Frank Frisch?" the man asked.

"Frisch?" the Flash asked rhetorically, a natural mimic, raising his brow in mock puzzlement. "Never heard of him."

When McGraw learned that Frisch wasn't there, he was hurt and angry. The Flash had jumped the club. NO player could do that to Little Napoleon, especially HIS boy. Hadn't the writers often referred to Frisch as "McGraw's boy?" And the ungrateful pup would do this to him. Just wait till John J. got back to New York!

When the Giants returned to New York, Frisch was incommunicado in the Bronx, reportedly ill, not only because McGraw announced he had been fined $500. The Flash was remorseful, but stubborn. He was riding two charley horses, knife-like pains in the hamstrings of the legs, and he was still stung that McGraw had accused him of "trying to give the game away."

Finally, George Kelly got a call through to Ada that the Old Man wanted to see Frank. So Frisch reported to the Polo Grounds. Neither man would apologize, but the player insisted, "That $500 fine is out." McGraw parried, "We'll see."

Years later, Frisch would say that when he left the clubhouse to work out, he knew that his days with the Giants were numbered. He would agree, too, with newspaper speculation that he'd blown his chance to succeed McGraw as manager.

Still, even though hitting .314 in 135 of the Giants' 154 games as the ball club finished fifth, the first time lower than second place in ten years, Frisch was good for one last blow. The final weekend of the season he hit a tenth-inning home run, righthanded, off Cincinnati's Eppa Rixey to knock the Reds out of first place, just before the Cardinals clinched the pennant at the Polo Grounds.

ST. LOUIS' first National League pennant ever was the old French fur-trading post's first success since Chris Von der Ahe's old St. Louis Browns. The Browns were managed by Charley Comiskey to four straight American Association pennants (1885-88) when the Association was classified as a major league. It was a victory for the have-nots and the home-growns.

The man of the hour of the 1926 Cardinals was that good-looking, dimple-cheeked second baseman-manager. The Rajah, Rogers Hornsby, had slipped at bat to .317 in his first full season as field foreman from those five previous magnificent years: .397, .401, .384, .424 and .403.

He still was THE hero, even more than Old Pete Alexander, who had contributed twelve regular-season victories, then won two and saved one in a World Series upset over the Yankees. The Cardinals hadn't stopped Babe Ruth. But, although the Babe would hit four home runs, including three in one game, Hornsby's pitchers often cagily walked him.

So the Series came down to the seventh game in which Alexander, sleepy-eyed from sitting up much of the night with a sick bottle, sauntered in from the bullpen in the seventh inning, protecting a one-run lead, 3-2. With bases loaded, two out, Alex struck out rookie Tony Lazzeri. Then, in the ninth, after he narrowly had walked Ruth on a full-count pitch, the Babe foolishly tried to steal second.

A surprising bid, all right, but a rare Ruthian misjudgment. Alexander used a short-armed delivery, which got the ball to the plate quickly. The catcher, Bob O'Farrell, had a powerful throwing arm. He gunned the ball to Hornsby at second base.

The hard-bitten Texan had ordered his mother's funeral held up so he could finish the Series. He slapped the ball on the Babe in what Rog constantly would call "the greatest thrill of my life."

St. Louis went berserk with the wildest demonstration since the 1918 Armistice. They renamed a street for Hornsby and gave the superstar-manager a new car, which he promptly lost at the gambling tables. Rog didn't drink or smoke, but he loved fast horses and hot dice.

For all his success, however, when feuding with Branch Rickey, the general manager he'd succeeded as field manager on Memorial Day,

1925, Hornsby finally had alienated Sam Breadon, the Cardinals' club-owner. Down the stretch in '26, the manager had asked Breadon to cancel an exhibition game at New Haven, Connecticut, so that his bone-weary ball players would have a day off.

Breadon picked the moment after a defeat to walk into the Cardinals' clubhouse to tell Hornsby that he'd tried, but failed. The New Haven club operator, George Weiss, had said he'd spent a considerable amount in promotion.

Hornsby reddened Breadon's face, squared the Irishman's jaw and brought the boss stiffily erect with wounded pride. As the *St. Louis Post-Dispatch's* gifted J. Roy Stockton put it, with originality and delicacy that the outspoken Hornsby couldn't match, Mr. Blunt "recommended an utterly impossible disposition of the exhibition game."

Breadon spun on his heel and left. When Hornsby in the moment of his greatest triumph asked for a three-year contract at $50,000 each, some said Breadon was too frugal to tie himself up for that long a period. Others said that, coldly, Singin' Sam, the barbershop man, knew exactly what he was doing, i.e., making Hornsby an offer he KNEW the manager would refuse.

October dragged into November. Then Thanksgiving gave way for the Christmas rush. Everyone was jolly in St. Louis except out there at 3623 Dodier Street, the ball park office of the Cardinals. Hornsby and Breadon hassled. B.R., angry when kicked upstairs to general manager as Breadon turned over the team on the field to Hornsby, had sold his Cardinals' stock. Breadon had arranged for Rog to buy it, endorsing the new manager's note of $50,000 for the $30,000 par-value holdings.

Rickey had done pretty well making a profit, but the stock had soared with the ball club. So B.R. couldn't be happy, but, bless his bushy brows, he was displeased more by the continued arrogance of that profane Hornsby. He knew what Rog felt about the football-style blackboard chalk-talks Branch had given as manager. Hornsby's first action had been to throw out the blackboard. To Hornsby, the "business manager," as he insisted on demeaning the GM, was an unnecessary nuisance between the field manager and the clubowner.

Bringing grins from writers who traveled with the Cardinals, the slugger from Hornsby Bend, Texas, referred to the Bible-quoting, polysyllabic Michigan law-school graduate, by way of Ohio Wesleyan, as that "Ohio Weez-lee-un bustard" or the sounds-like equivalent thereof.

Rickey always had his yes-men and eavesdroppers. He knew. Now that the Cardinals were champions, he advised Breadon that they could afford to deal Hornsby. William Wrigley at Chicago had offered cash, as much as New York, but money wouldn't do now. The fans wouldn't stand for it. The Cardinals couldn't stand the playing-field loss.

The Cardinals had stung the Giants with a trading-deadline deal in '26, giving up B.R.'s pet, an innocent home-town character named Clarence (Heinie) Mueller for veteran outfield stabilizer Billy Southworth. Now maybe they could get Frisch for Hornsby—Frisch, a couple of years younger than Rog. Maybe the Giants would throw in that big first-base kid they hadn't used much in '26, Bill Terry?

Breadon nodded. He'd try, aware he was unloosing the devil dogs, but the one-time poor boy who had skinny-dipped in New York's East River had heart and a high regard for that crooked-nose cat from home, Frisch.

When Sam wondered if the Giants still were interested in Hornsby, they were indeed, and a bit surprised. The baseball grapevine had said that all was not well between Breadon and his player-manager, but still . . .

Yes, said Stoneham quickly. McGraw was now in the mood to give up Frisch, but no, Mac wouldn't include Terry. Besides, what did St. Louis want with a first baseman when the Cardinals had Jim Bottomley?

Negotiations were suspended, and Breadon met again with Hornsby in a stormy session. Next, he met with his Odd Couple counterpart. A peach of a pair: Sam, the elbow-tilting, big-city Irishman, a barbershop-harmony Democrat, and Branch, a psalm-singing, small-town teetotaling Republican.

That day, December 21, 1926, Rickey stepped outside Breadon's office to find a visitor, Warren Giles, a St. Joseph, Missouri, ball club operator he had just convinced Breadon to hire to run the Cardinals' new top farm club at Syracuse, New York.

Dramatically, Rickey gnawed at a cigar and said, solemnly, "Warren, my future—and the Cardinals'—might be decided in that office in the next few minutes."

It was, quickly. Breadon got Stoneham on the phone. "Charley," he said, "Hornsby is yours for Frisch and (pitcher) Jimmy Ring."

Minutes later, Breadon emerged, nodded to Rickey, and, speaking obliquely with Giles present, the clubowner said, "It's done, Branch."

Who could know whether it was the beginning of the end—or the end of the beginning?

8

Dethroning the Rajah

IT WAS April, 1927 in St. Louis. A long-gone downtown department store, Nugent's, was advertising silk dresses at two for $5 and mahagony four-poster beds for $19.75. You could get a new Ford for $471.87, a Chevy comparably, and a Pontiac Six, if you wanted to splurge, for $745.

Round steak was eighteen cents a pound, hamburger sixteen cents, and Frank Frisch felt like the biggest hamburger of them all.

The Cardinals were playing their city rivals, the American League Browns, managed by George Sisler, the great first baseman. Bob O'Farrell's Redbirds just had railroaded in from their last spring-training stop, Nashville, Tennessee, where they'd evened an eight-game exhibition series with their 1926 World Series rivals, the New York Yankees.

Sure, the Babe had hit one at Sulphur Dell, that quaint Nashville bandbox ball park, but they'd offered a $20 prize for anyone who'd hit the ball over a laundry sign on the outfield fence. And Frank Frisch, the money player, had had a field day. He'd won the "Andrew Jackson." In addition, teeing off on Bob Shawkey and Myles Thomas as if he were the Sultan of Swat himself, he'd had two doubles AND two home runs.

O'Farrell, the National League's Most Valuable Player as catcher of the 1926 world champions, had been named manager to replace Rogers Hornsby. O'Farrell, wearing the new Redbird uniform shirt with the proud words in black—"World Champions" girdling a single chipper Cardinal—spoke reassuringly of the controversial December deal, Hornsby for Frisch.

"I believe," said the round-faced blond with the schoolgirl complexion and baby-blue eyes, "that we gained something in speed, ground-covering ability and double-play efficiency."

No one in his right mind would label Frisch a better hitter than Hornsby, and some, like Frank's old friend, Casey Stengel, would question that "double play efficiency," too. On the DP, Rog "cheated" toward second base so that he could approach the bag facing directly toward third and cut the ball across his chest in a one-movement flip. Frankie, although strong-armed, needed an extra step in getting the ball away, perhaps to grip the horsehide better because of that deformed middle finger.

Pop flies? Well, there was really no comparison. Frisch was a fourth outfielder, ranging all over the place. Hornsby struggled backing up to catch a fly ball from second base.

Quipped Frisch in recollection, "Rog always felt the right fielder was paid to do something, too." Uh-huh, and the center fielder, also.

Roy Stockton, a Hornsby man who became an early convert to Frisch's personality and play, had a dry explanation for the Rajah's weakness on pop-ups. "Because," wrote Stockton, "Hornsby was unfamiliar with them. He hit so few himself . . . "

Unquestionably, Frisch covered more ground with greater quickness and range, but, as mentioned, the Flash felt like sixteen-cents-a-pound hamburger that first game in the Cardinals' uniform. The Browns filled the bases in the first inning. Sisler slapped a sharp grounder to the Flash, who realized he'd have to work rapidly to turn it into a double play.

So with the typical squat he used to field ground balls, Frankie reached down and, as fielding malfeasance once was described by *The Washington Post's* Shirley Povich, he felt nothing. Despite Frisch's body-blocking defensive technique, the ball slithered through his chunky legs for a two-run error.

Frisch didn't raise his head. Hands on his knees, he heard the caterwaul, loud and clear:

"We want Hornsby . . . WE WANT HORNSBY . . . "

No trade perhaps was ever so provocative as the one that proved a

Christmas grinch for so many baseball fans, especially in St. Louis. Of course, Frisch had his faithful in New York, but Frankie didn't have the fanatical following of Hornsby, the .400 hitting 1925 MVP who just had piloted the lowly Cardinals to that long-awaited first championship.

The joke—and joker—in the deal was Jimmy Ring. By then a journeyman pitcher, thirty-two years old, he humphed that he didn't think he'd report to St. Louis. Who cared? He'd been 11-10 with the Giants in '26, with a whopping 4.57 earned-run average. And, in fact, when he did report to the Cardinals, he was 0-and-4 in thirteen games with a 6.35 ERA—and gone.

Frisch didn't want to leave New York. Truth is, St. Louis really didn't want him. When Breadon, whose courage, cash and Rickey's brains had built the perennial also-rans from pretenders to contenders, announced that startling deal, the unusual happened.

The St. Louis Chamber of Commerce denounced Breadon in a resolution. Unhappy unknowns festooned the front door of the club-owner's fashionable home with black crepe. They also draped his Pierce-Arrow automobile agency funerally. One sports editor, Jim Gould of *The St. Louis Star,* wrote angrily that he would never cover another Cardinal ballgame.

Gould admired Hornsby, including Rog's addiction to dice, and line drives to right center. Jim had covered the Rajah regularly, including 1924 when Hornsby had established the Twentieth Century's highest batting average, .424.

Hornsby didn't want to leave St. Louis, his adopted home, and he stated his case eloquently, further stirring the cannibal's pot in which Breadon boiled. Finally resigned, Rog accepted a $40,000 contract from the Giants as second baseman and McGraw's managerial assistant, but that stock he held in the Cardinals was a gilt-edged security of a different color.

Hornsby wanted $130,000 for the stock for which he'd paid just $50,000 only a year and a half earlier. Breadon bowed his neck at $80,000. The commissioner, Judge Landis, had a quaint notion that a stockholder in the St. Louis club couldn't play second base for New York.

The impasse wasn't broken until almost opening day when National League president, John Heydler, convinced NL teams to pony up $5,000 each to make up the difference between what Breadon had offered and Hornsby demanded. Rog's stock would be retired.

Frisch, meanwhile, talked briefly of quitting. But heck, this was 1927. Ball players hadn't found King Solomon's mines or the treasure of the Sierra Madre in the legal ruling that later buried the corset-binding reserve clause. Frankie didn't have the money to retire although he'd been pretty well paid for his day, and he didn't have the freedom.

So, suddenly, he quit whining. He got his Dutch up. Okay, so McGraw wouldn't let bygones be bygones. Frankie would show him and those show-me buzzards out there in that hot hell-hole, St. Louis. He

Fit as Favorite Fiddle:
Frank Frisch, angry and
eager, worked out daily in-
doors and outdoors for his
greatest challenge, replac-
ing Rogers Hornsby in St.
Louis.

took dear Ada, and went up to Lake Placid, where the gifted athlete skied, skated and ran daily. When he did nothing else to turn that twenty-nine-year-old body into its best condition ever, he'd take his dogs and go out to romp in the snow or sit outside and read.

In January, Branch Rickey, visiting Syracuse to inspect International League farm facilities there, invited Frisch to come up. B.R. wanted a look-see and to add nickel-on-the-drum inspiration. He needn't have bothered.

"Mr. Rickey," said Frisch, firmly, "tell Mr. Breadon I'm in the best shape I've ever been in."

At Avon Park, Florida, where the Cardinals trained then, the world champions were naturally a bit cool toward the Flash as the man who'd replaced their leader, the Rajah. But, it was hard not to like the Dutchman.

They KNEW he was a great ball player. He was friendly, too. And, although he knew all the bad words as well as the good ones, he didn't flout his knowledge. He'd played violin and still plunked a ukelele, the instrument of the high-life Twenties. He really preferred the ponderous, full-orchestra Germanic longhair music of Wagner, meaning Richard, not Honus. But he could do his thing with "Yes, Sir, That's My Baby" and "Bye-Bye Blackbird."

Music Man: Soothed and pleased by music throughout his life, Frisch shows a bit of skill back home when he was still young and a Giant in 1922.

He liked to dance and, obviously, was light on his feet. He liked a little Prohibition schnapps as well as heimgemach, i.e., home brew. Now and then, he'd like a little too much, but drinking was a social delight more than a necessity with Frisch.

He'd talk politics, if necessary, although he preferred to talk about cutting a steak or the cutoff play of the ball field, instead of cutting the economy. A trifle conservative, he leaned toward Republicans. He liked it that high-collared Herbert Hoover, announced presidential candidate, was a good baseball fan.

To veteran Cardinals, accustomed to the New York accent of club-owner Sam Breadon, who'd gone from bank clerk in the Big Apple to grease monkey and then auto-agency operator in St. Louis, it was amusing to hear the boss and the new field captain talk about the ball club. Both referred to it as the "Cawd'nals."

Frisch didn't talk fishing as much as some of the southern fellas, but he'd tracked a moose in heavy snow, which impressed the club's hunters. He didn't know as much about farming as Sunny Jim Bottomley or about chicken-raising as soft-spoken Chick Hafey, whose nickname came from his business hobby in California. But he knew more than any about flora and fauna. As a horticulturist, he had a green thumb almost as talented as Ada's. And he could talk ornithology with his friend from *The New York Times,* John Kieran, later a walking "Information Please" encyclopedia on radio and television.

Basically, though, Frisch was just one of the boys, less a loner than Hornsby. Soon he was accepted by the 1927 Cardinals, who were aware that he was, indeed, the man on the spot marked "X."

Imagine whipping up the Hornsby-versus-Frisch rivalry to the point that the press even displayed the respective exhibition batting averages daily. For the record, the Flash hit .376 that spring of '27. The Rajah hit .365.

Then, as mentioned, when O'Farrell brought his Birds back home from the South, that first ground ball rolled right through Frisch's legs, bringing that we-want-Hornsby chant from the stands. Frankie felt as if the spot marked "X" was truly a hot spot.

YEARS LATER, Frisch would remember that moment as snake-belly low. For a guy who could waver from almost head-hanging, aw-shucks shyness to bragadoccio, if only the good-natured kind of hey-they-forgot-the-Flash-did-this-or-that, Frankie would omit the climax of that curtain-raising embarrassment at St. Louis.

The same day he gave away two first-inning runs to the Browns, he reclaimed them by winning the game for Jesse Haines, and the Cardinals, 5-3, by belting one in the eighth.

That's the kind of year it was for Frisch in 1927. He didn't make them forget Hornsby, but rather, remember Frisch.

Opening day, facing the Chicago Cubs' hard-throwing Pat Malone, who'd knock down his mother if not grandma, the Flash belted a triple and homer for a 4-3 victory at Sportsman's Park. That day the Cards lined up with Taylor Douthit, center field; Watty Holm, third base; Frisch, second base; Bottomley, first base; Hafey, right field; Wally Roettger, left field; Tommy Thevenow, shortstop; O'Farrell, catcher, and Bill Sherdel, pitcher.

If that lineup had stayed intact, chances are that the Cardinals would have romped off with a pennant and Frisch would have earned a well-deserved Most Valuable Player award. That day after doing in the Cubs, for instance, he tripled twice to beat Cincinnati. He was a whirling dervish on the field and bases.

At Philadelphia, he scored the winning run on a popped-up "sacrifice" fly just behind the infield. He scored from second base on fly balls and infield outs, from first base on a single. Afield, he was everywhere. Once, in counter-action to an enemy surprise sacrifice bunt, the Flash raced to first from his position at second, slid in feet first and took a putout throw in a sitting position.

Defensively, working behind Pete Alexander, or "Old Low and Away," as Haines called Alex, and behind good ol' Jess, whose knuckler also dipped, Frisch found himself with more ground-ball chances than he'd ever seen.

Frisch teamed with Swiss-watch timing around second base with Thevenow. "Tommy," he would recall years later, "was the best shortstop I ever played with when it came to feeding you the ball, consistently chest high, for the double-play pivot."

But just about the same time manager O'Farrell went out with a broken thumb, Thevenow suffered a broken ankle in a slide, prompting a disastrous medley relay at shortstop. George (Specs) Toporcer, Les Bell, Heinie Schuble, Rabbit Maranville, and even Frisch himself paraded to that sensitive defensive position. The Flash in one game.

The bulk of the responsibility fell on twenty-year-old Schuble, called up from Danville, Illinois in the Class B Three-I League. The leap was too great. Heine was nervous and jittery. More than once when the kid made a critical error, Frisch would put a protective arm around him as they left the field, trying to settle down the kid.

Meanwhile, making plays on BOTH sides of second base, Frisch handled 1037 chances, a record intact for all major league infielders except, naturally, first basemen. The Dutchman was proud of that mark, a tribute to his quickness, ground-gobbling and efficiency. The glove he used in 1927, incredibly worn, is part of the Flash's display at the Baseball Hall of Fame in Cooperstown, New York.

At bat, establishing a St. Louis record for fewest strikeouts, ten, in 617 official times at bat, Frisch hit .337, fourth-highest of his career. He had 208 hits, including thirty-one doubles, eleven triples, ten homers and drove in seventy-eight runs. And as he would complain afterward, if he hadn't jammed his right wrist into a runner in early September, swelling the wrist virtually to the width of his hand, his average would have stayed closer to Hornsby's, which it did most of the season in daily newspaper comparisons.

At New York, the Rajah had a normal Hornsby season, i.e., .361, twenty-five homers and 125 RBIs, brilliant totals. But he chafed at the ink Frisch got, especially when the Fordham Flash stole forty-eight bases, a Redbird record until Lou Brock.

Once in St. Louis, the taller, huskier Hornsby offered the press that he would bet $1,000 he could beat Frisch down to first base or circling the bases. The story received good play. Frisch handled it gracefully. He laughed, "No, thanks, I'll save my running for the ball games. Besides, I think Rog is probably right."

Competitively, Hornsby never saw the day he could rise to an occasion better than Frisch.

When the Cardinals gave out their world championship rings in New York's first visit, the Flash discreetly stayed in the background as America's biggest hero of the moment, Col. Charles A. Lindbergh, the twenty-six-year-old former airmail pilot who just made the first solo 'flight to Paris in the "Spirit of St. Louis," did the honors as part of the

Young Lindy and Old Pete: *Charles A. Lindbergh, 26, the just-returned hero from a historic first transatlantic solo flight, presents 1926 world championship rings to the Cardinals. From left to right are Judge Landis (back to camera), Lindbergh, beaming high-collared baseball secretary Leslie O'Connor, bow-tied umpire Charley Moran, manager Bob O'Farrell, and Grover Cleveland (Old Pete) Alexander, hero of the World Series, shaking hands with Lindbergh.*

city's celebration. That day, before a packed house, Frisch outplayed Hornsby.

He did it again on "Hornsby Day" before a crowd of 20,000 that came out to pay tribute to the departed super-star. Rog went hitless and erred. Frisch doubled and stole a base.

So it was in the pennant race. Winning ninety-two games, three more than the Cardinals had taken the year before, O'Farrell's Redbirds finished a half-game ahead of McGraw's Giants in 1927. And in voting for the National League MVP, Frisch finished second to Pittsburgh's Paul Waner with sixty-six points to Waner's seventy-two. Hornsby was third with fifty-four. Frisch, in view of the pressure and performance deserved this award more than one he received later.

In '27, Haines won twenty-four games and Alexander, past forty, won twenty-one. But the Cardinals were nosed out by Pittsburgh, for which Waner had hit .380.

The end came, perhaps just as well, on September 29, the day a killer tornado, second worst in St. Louis history, devastated the city. It ripped the pavilion roof off Sportsman's park, dumping the twisted wood and steel into Grand Avenue. The center field flagpole was torn down, toppling onto the playing field. Iron girders were bent.

At Cincinnati that very day, although Frisch homered, little Redleg lefthander Jakie May handed Redbird rookie righthander Fred Frankhouse his only defeat in six decisions, 3-2. The Cardinals were eliminated from the race.

"I guess," said Frisch, "we'd have had a helluva time trying to play a World Series in the ball park, but, dammit, if Rickey had brought up Maranville a couple of weeks earlier from Rochester, we'd have done it. The Rabbit was crazy, but, man, he could play shortstop."

Frisch, himself, all-round, had never been better. Not even in 1923 when Sam Crane, pioneer big leaguer and long-time New York writer, labeled him "the best fielder and consistent hitter I ever saw." Or when the second baseman the Flash so admired, Eddie Collins, then playing with the Chicago Americans, observed after a post-season 1924 tour with the Giants to the British Isles:

"Frisch, I think, is the best ball player in the National League. As a fielder, base runner and hitting either way, slugging or bunting, the best compliment I can pay Frank is that he is the Sisler of the National League."

Frisch, in turn, regarded Sisler, the Brown's first baseman, and Babe Ruth, the Yankee outfielder, as the best players he ever saw.

"The rapier and the cannon," the Flash would say later, in pretty good imagery. "George was the perfect player, poetry in motion. The Babe, hell, he made the big leagues look like high school. He could pitch and bat fourth."

In the post-season of the crippled Cardinals' near-miss in 1927, the Flash returned home to the Bronx, where New York sports writer Ed

Sullivan, who would win a greater reputation as host of television's long-running variety show, "Toast of the Town," hailed the Flash.

"He showed 'em," wrote Sullivan. "It was, Frank said, the best season he had defensively and could have been his best offensively if he hadn't been hurt and hadn't moved up to second in the batting order, cutting down his runs batted in. But he was particularly pleased with the way St. Louis fans treated him. 'They were just fine,' he said, 'though you couldn't blame them for resenting the trade of Hornsby.'"

The plain-talking Texan, Hornsby, en route to playing for four clubs in four years, lasted only one season in the Polo Grounds despite heavy hitting. He tongue-lashed traveling secretary Jim Tierney for second-guessing. He angered owner Charley Stoneham and even displeased McGraw.

When Mac was away, leaving the Rajah in charge, third baseman Fred Lindstrom hesitated in an infield drill to make certain second was covered by Hornsby before cutting loose the ball. Rog chewed him out.

"But," protested young Lindy, "that's the way the Old Man wants us to do it—to make certain we get one (force out)."

Said Hornsby brusquely, "When the Old Man's here, do it his way. I'm in charge now. Do it my way."

At least one New York writer, Richards Vidmer, learned early that Hornsby would call them as he saw them, regardless. On the spring train carrying the Giants back to New York, Vidmer wondered how the manager of the 1926 World champion Cardinals saw the '27 Giants? Could they win the pennant?

"Not," said Hornsby, bluntly, "with Farrell at shortstop." Eddie (Doc) Farrell was seated next to Rog at a dining-car table.

In January, 1928, the Giants traded Rogers Hornsby to the Boston Braves in a woeful mismatch. As outfielder Jimmy Welsh and catcher Frank (Shanty) Hogan came, McGraw was discreetly far from the questioning, indignant press. He vacationed in his favorite recreation spot, Havana.

By then, both Sam Breadon, and Branch Rickey could congratulate themselves—and Frisch—with a sigh of relief. If, as Frisch once said, his top playing pay was $28,000 before the Depression made fewer dollars available for all, it's probable the reward came because of 1927.

In the Flash's scrapbooks at Cooperstown is a letter written to him in early October, 1927, by Rickey. B.R. apologized for not having had a chance to say thanks, personally, writing:

"I wanted you to know how deeply and genuinely I appreciate the fine effort you made. I want to tell that nothing has been more gratifying than your attitude. You are not only to be congratulated on the character of your play, but the great influence for good sportsmanship . . .

"This is not simply a formal note of appreciation, but is meant to be just a little personal expression of my own high regard for you as a player and as a man. It would not be necessary for us to have men of your playing ability in all positions to win a pennant, but it would be most gratifying if we had men of your caliber and character and spirit whether we ever won a pennant. I look forward next year to another pleasant and profitable season and another great year for you.

"I hope we are set to fight every inch of the way for the pennant and I believe that a few changes we contemplate will add geatly to our strength . . . "

Breadon, who openly embraced Frisch after the season, realized that the Cardinals' home attendance had improved from 681,575 to a club record 763,615, en route to a 1928 high of 778,147. That would endure until prosperity after World War II made the million-gate become commonplace.

Ill in 1947, Breadon sold out. When dying of cancer two years later, he was asked to look back to nearly thirty seasons' association with the Cardinals, to nine pennants, six world championship ball clubs. Maybe he'd pick an All-Star team?

"I couldn't do that," said the pain-wracked man. "Take left field alone. In virtual succession, I had Chick Hafey, Joe Medwick and Stan Musial. But I'll tell you this. The greatest single-season player I had was Frank Frisch in 1927.

"Just as I was certain that night baseball would make every day Sunday, I was sure—after Frisch's success in Hornsby's spot and the way the fans warmed up to Frank—that it was the team that counted, the pennant race and not the individual.

"I never again was afraid to trade a ball player."

Rags Before Riches: *An unlikely pair in success, Branch Rickey (center) and Sam Breadon (right) looked even more unseemly at spring training in 1922 when the Cardinals were still rag-tag. Huddling with Rickey is traveling secretary Clarence F. Lloyd.*

Ladies Day Favorite: *A swaggering southpaw, cap-tilted Sunny Jim Bottomley, the naive country boy who made it big as a Hall of Fame first baseman with the Cardinals.*

9
Of Friends—and Foes

I'M NINETEEN years old and I love to play ball and . . . "

That's the way the letter began, written to Branch Rickey in 1920 from a mining and farming community, Nokomis, Illinois.

Sometimes, as they say, it pays to be good and lucky. Rickey answered that letter. James Leroy Bottomley, a crackerbarrel philosopher with a name that sounded more like a British butler, became one of the best bargains the Redbirds ever got.

After all, you couldn't beat the price for signing a future Most Valuable Player, and Hall of Famer—zip. Signing Bottomley proved to be a good move for the Cardinals; one of many changes that improved the Cardinals' 1928 line-up.

Watching a spring-training workout in Florida with Sid Keener, long-time St. Louis sports editor, Rickey heard a bat crack a ball with remarkable resonance. The ball leaped over B.R.'s head as he strolled in the outfield.

"By Judas Priest," he exclaimed, "who hit that ball?"

"Chick Hafey," said coach Burt Shotton. "Hafey—a pitcher."

"No sir," roared Rickey. "You mean FORMERLY a pitcher. I want that young man tried in the outfield."

So Charles (Chick) Hafey became the first bespectacled batting champion, and, like Bottomley, a Hall of Famer.

Hafey was another player responsible for the Cardinals' improvement in 1928. The ninety-five games the club won that season was the most for a team that had been in-and-out of the National League since the charter season, 1876, the year Custer lost his command and life at the Little Big Horn.

Customarily, on the eight pennant-winning ball clubs on which Frank Frisch played, the Flash was the "big man," until age began to take its toll. But in 1928, although he hit .300 and drove in eighty-six runs, he was outstripped offensively by Bottomley and Hafey. And a University of Illinois rookie outfielder named Wally Roettger was going great with .346 until he broke a leg sliding in mid-season. He was never the same.

Fortunately for the Cardinals' pennant chances, Rickey had shored up the outfield in a May trade that brought thirty-six-year-old lefthanded-hitting outfield veteran, George Washington Harper, from the New York Giants. B.R. dispatched the Cardinals' former manager, catcher Bob O'Farrell.

Curiously, Sam Breadon hadn't been impressed with O'Farrell's managing even though the ball club in 1927 had won three games more than in 1926. As mentioned, it had lost shortstop Tommy Thevenow with a career-crippling broken ankle. O'Farrell had wound up with a broken thumb that cut his catching from 146 to 53.

Breadon rewarded O'Farrell with a $5,000 pay hike for taking a demotion. The clubowner promoted Bill McKechnie, scholarly coach who had won a world championship at Pittsburgh in 1925. And then when O'Farrell played inadequately in early-season play, he went to the Giants for Harper.

Harper, a lefthanded hitter, was necessary because Breadon and Rickey had sent Frisch's former New York teammate, peppery little Billy Southworth, to Rochester to manage the top farm club that had been moved from Syracuse.

With O'Farrell gone, Rickey swung a deal the next day that went a long way to solidifying the Cardinals in 1928 and for future big seasons. He sent rookie catcher Virgil (Spud) Davis, outfielder Homer Peel and cash to Philadelphia for catcher Jimmy Wilson.

Wilson, a Philadelphian with jet-black hair, swarthy complexion and fascinating green eyes, was a smart hombre who could move well despite thick, soccer-developed legs. Pretty good hitter, too, even if he didn't bat highly in 1928.

"Ace," his nickname, did what the pitching-minded defense-oriented McKechnie wanted. He handled that pitching staff on which Haines again won twenty games, and ancient Alexander won sixteen. Lefty

Ace's High: Jimmy Wilson, called "Ace," was the key man acquired by Branch Rickey in 1928 to catch the Cardinals' low-ball pitching staff.

Wee Willie Sherdel slow-balled and quick-pitched his way to a staff-leading 21-10 record.

Frisch, relieved to be allowed to run on his own again, but not by the a marionette-manipulating McGraw, voluntarily reduced his stolen-base total to twenty-nine.

"I probably could have run more," said the Flash who, like Jackie Robinson later, would paw the dirt with his back (left) foot at first base to agitate and annoy opposing pitchers even when he wasn't going.

"But the way Bottomley and Hafey were hitting in the number four and number five spots in the batting order, it didn't make good sense to take the risk or to distract them," Flash said. "I'd usually go only in a low-scoring game when we were having trouble with a pitcher or maybe with the score tied in a late inning."

Sunny Jim and Chick were as unalike as their backgrounds and personalities. Bottomley, cap cocked at a rakish angle on the left side of his head, was a swaggering, Ladies' Day favorite. A six-foot, 175-pound lefthander the country boy from Nokomis became a most eligible bachelor.

By then, using a choked grip, unusual for a power hitter, and wiggling his bat with almost deceptively slow nonchalance, he had his moments, after reporting so naively to his first Cardinals' spring training. There, he fingered a long, broomstick-thin bat, looked at the label and drawled, "Who's this Mr. Fungo?"

By 1923, just his second season in the majors, the twenty-three-year-old Bottomley hit .371. Once he hit seven home runs over a five-game period, and twice he had six hits in a game, including September 16, 1924 at Brooklyn, where he set the astonishing record of twelve runs batted in—in one game, not a week.

In 1925, Sunny Jim had 227 hits, including a league-leading forty-four doubles, twelve triples and twenty-one homers, driving in 128 runs in a .367 season. And then in '28 he won the National League's Most Valuable Player award and the $1,000 bag of gold that then went with it. Quite a grand sight: a sack full of $5 gold pieces plunked down on home plate in pre-game ceremonies.

Bottomley, then twenty-eight, batted .325 that season, but it was his production that caught the eye of baseball MVP electors. He scored 123 runs and drove in 136. Almost half (93) of his 187 hits were for extra bases. He hit forty-two doubles, led the league in triples with twenty and tied Chicago's Hack Wilson with thirty-one home runs.

Sunny Jim, who also loved to hunt and fish, had rural wit and philosophy to go with that easy-does-it smile and manner.

Said first-base rival Bill Terry, helping vote Jim into the baseball Hall of Fame as a member of Cooperstown's Veterans' Committee:

"Frisch was tough in a pinch, but on those early St. Louis champions, it was Bottomley that we (the Giants) feared the most."

Frisch nodded. "And a great guy on a ball club," he said. "I remember one time when we weren't playing up to our par and Doc Weaver (trainer) talked up the need for a long winning streak.

"Jim said, 'Naw, Doc, that ain't the way to win a pennant. Just win two, lose one, win two, lose one . . . until you get to about 100—and then throw the rest of 'em away.'"

That's about the way a close three-way race with John McGraw's

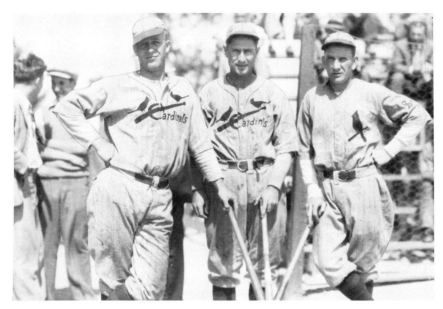

Lucky Rabbit: Walter (Rabbit) Maranville, who played big league baseball until he was 44, wears a rumpled, single Redbird uniform of 1927. From the left, Jim Bottomley, utility infielder-outfielder Roscoe (Watty) Holm, and the former pixilated pixy, Maranville.

New York Giants and Joe McCarthy's Chicago Cubs went in 1928. And Hafey, four years younger, taller, rangier than Bottomley, was a rawboned righthanded hitter who pulled the ball savagely and came into his own to help considerably.

Extremely fast and strong-armed, Chick had moved to left field, deeper at 351 down the line than the 310-foot barrier at the fence in St. Louis' right field. The idea, of course, was to permit the quicker, better outfielder to cover more ground. But if he'd ever played right field, he would have at least thrown out a batter occasionally at first base or made the foe move up cautiously, a base at a time.

St. Louis' little third baseman, Andy High, obtained from Boston just before the '28 season so that slump-shackled Les Bell could rejoin old mentor Rogers Hornsby, would crinkle with an octogenarian's smile when he remembered Hafey and one of Rickey's favorite reclamation projects, thirty-seven-year-old shortstop Rabbit Maranville.

"With those belt-high basket catches, the kind Willie Mays made later, Rabbit was good and colorful, the steady shortstop the club had needed the year before to team with Frisch," recalled High. "And he had an uncanny knack of moving himself and me to the wrong spot that turned out to be just right."

High concurred with the National League's premier third baseman, Pie Traynor, that Hafey hit the ball harder down the third-base line than any other batter. In '28, after taking over two years earlier when Ray Blades ruined his career by severely wrenching his knee in a collision with the outfield wall, Chick came up with a .337 season. In just 138 games, belting forty-six doubles and twenty-seven homers, he drove in 111 runs.

"Look at his career, the high percentage of runs batted in for games played," said High, "but he couldn't play every day because the bad case of sinusitis he'd get in mid-summer. It would almost blind him. Helped when he went to glasses, but we still missed him when he was out."

The foe didn't, however. Most certainly not former Philadelphia and Brooklyn infielder, witty Fresco Thompson.

In one memorable game, Hafey smashed a double painfully off Thompson's shins at third base. Next time, the Berkeley, California athlete saw Thompson playing quite deep. Chick bunted toward third and easily beat the play.

The next inning, when the Cardinals batted again, a young vendor leaned over the side of the dugout, extending an ice cream bar and called to Hafey.

"Mr. Hafey, please," the kid called out, finally getting the quiet outfielder's attention. "Compliments of Mr. Thompson. And if you bunt again, he said he'll send another one."

High recalled a critical play made at the finish of a race won by just two games over New York in the Giants' last gasp under McGraw. High drove in the tying run at Boston with a ninth-inning single off Bob Smith, but in the fourteenth, against the seventh-place club managed by a familiar name, Rogers Hornsby, it looked all over.

One more former Redbird, Jack Smith, was on second base when ex-Cardinal Heine Mueller singled to left. Hafey cut loose an incredible throw to the plate to nip Smith, and save the game.

Harper's three home runs in one game had salvaged a critical contest at the Polo Grounds. In the fifteenth at Boston, he lifted a flyball dropped by Lance Richbourg. The Braves folded. Frisch stole home.

The pennant was clinched the next day when Sherdel, aided by Flint Rhem, beat Boston, 3-1, as New York lost to Chicago, 7-5. A 52-23 record on the road, including eleven out of fifteen on the last swing, put McKechnie's team into the World Series.

THE CARDINALS were favored over the New York Yankees in the Series, even though the Yanks were world champions. In 1927, having won 110 games, they had murdered Pittsburgh four straight. It was just that in '28, Miller Higgins had wound up with walking wounded.

Although they had won 101 games and Babe Ruth and Lou Gehrig had driven in 142 runs each, Hug needed a blue cross battery of Johnson and

Chicken Feed: *Rangy Charles (Chick) Hafey bought a six-wheeled midnight blue Auburn in 1929, then used it angrily to drive 90 miles across the desert from Florida to California two years later when the Cardinals wouldn't meet the Hall of Famer's salary demands as batting champion.*

Johnson for the Series, or McKesson and Robbins. Star lefthander Herb Pennock, who had beaten the Cardinals twice in the 1926 World Series, was out with a lame arm. The crack center fielder, fleet Earle Combs, was sidelined with cracked ribs. The second baseman, Tony Lazzeri, was so lame-armed that every time the Yankees were out in front, Hug would bench Tony for that fresh kid, Leo Durocher. Even the Babe himself was hobbling with a lame ankle.

What magnificent cripples—especially Ruth!

Gehrig? Heck, there was NEVER anything wrong with the young Iron Horse!

Between them, the Babe and Biscuit Pants, the wide-bottomed Gehrig, decimated the Cardinals. Frisch had seen nothing like it with the Giants. Ruth went ten for sixteen, including three doubles, three homers, four RBIs and a record .625 average. One of his homers cleared the pavilion roof, bounded across Grand Avenue and broke a Chevrolet showcase window. Blithely, the Babe went over afterward, propped a foot on a Chevy running board and autographed for a beaming proprietor and awed admirers.

Gehrig, hitting cleanup behind the Babe, was equally . . . well, judge for yourself: Six for eleven, .545, including a double, four homers and nine RBIs in just four games.

The scores were 4-1 and 9-3 at Yankee Stadium, 7-3 at Sportsman's Park and, again, 7-3.

Only the fourth game was really a contest. As late as the seventh inning Sherdel led Hoyt, 2-1. Then, standing on the mound, Sherry took a catcher's throw, and, using no battery sign, immediately threw it past Ruth for strike three.

The 37,331 crowd roared approval, but National League umpire, Cy Pfirman, working the plate, disallowed the quick pitch. Captain Frisch ran in from second base, Sherdel stormed down off the mound and McKechnie raced from the dugout. But the umpire was right. Before the Series, siding with the American League, Judge Landis had barred the quick pitch.

So, reprieved, Ruth belted his second homer of the game off Sherdel. Gehrig immediately teed off, too. An inning later, facing Alexander, who was bombed one way if not the other, the Babe hit his third homer of the game.

To climax a Series in which the Cardinals didn't hit, Ruth raced into the left-field bullpen, stuck his yellow glove into the crowd, made a fancy catch of the Frisch's foul, triumphantly held the ball aloft and pranced through the home dugout to the visitors' celebrating clubhouse.

En route back to New York, the Babe ripped off owner Jake Ruppert's pajama tops in a wild train trip. And manager Huggins tried to look dignified as he got off at Penn Station minus the false teeth he'd lost during the long night of liquid merriment.

For St. Louis, there was no joy. Breadon was so mortified that he fired pennant-winning manager, McKechnie, persuading Deacon Bill to swap jobs with Southworth at Rochester.

Andy High, walking past the Chase Hotel after the misery, bumped into the Giants' Bill Terry and Edd Roush, who told him the Cardinals had pitched Ruth wrong, throwing fast balls away from the Babe rather than breaking stuff down and in.

"Obviously we didn't pitch the Big Guy right," said High, dryly. (Privately, he wished they'd have walked Ruth more as Hornsby's staff had done two Series earlier.) "But we thought by throwing fast stuff away, we could keep him from pulling the ball into the pavilion, or onto the roof and beyond.

"You know what we probably would have done if we'd pitched the Babe down and in?"

"What?" chorused the two Giant stars.

"Killed Jim Bottomley at first base!"

10
Spirit of 1930

SAM BREADON, who changed managers as often as shirts, was in good spirits. It was August 17, 1930, a Monday open date. Singin' Sam, the barbershop man, toasted New York and St. Louis writers at his country place. Breadon liked the annual picnic because of his affection for both towns.

On that rare day in the first full year of the Depression, Breadon had just announced that Charles E. (Gabby) Street would manage the Cardinals again in 1931. Yes, even though, as in 1929, the Redbirds were a fourth-place ball club. And even though the boss had gone through five managers in five seasons.

In '29 they'd started fast under former teammate Billy Southworth. Some of the older players thought that Billy the Kid, none too gentle after a few drinks, had exercised more authority than necessary at times. Such as the time at spring training when he'd ordered the entire

79

Mr. Hyde: Although Billy (The Kid) Southworth, veteran hero of the 1926 world championship ball club, would return to the Cardinals to win three titles in the early 1940's, he was an uptight, gruff boss, battling both the bottle and former teammates in 1929.

ball club to take a train down from Avon Park to Miami. Jimmy Wilson had said that Mrs. Wilson, and little son Bobby were planning to motor down with him to see the moon over Miami.

"Drive," said Southworth sternly, "and it'll cost you $500."

Men with whom Billy had played with muttered mutinously, but Frank Frisch didn't get too excited. Hell, the Flash, like Southworth, had played for John McGraw. He knew that if it wasn't a hangover making Billy nasty, it had to be those years under McGraw. That's the way Mac would have done it—his way or else.

Frisch would have a good year in '29, hitting .334. But the Cardinals' pitching crashed like the stock market. Syl Johnson's 13-7 was the best on the staff. The worst, considering that Sherdel was 21-10 the year before, was Wee Willie's 10-15. And, at forty-two, Old Pete Alexander reached the end of the line with the Cardinals.

Frisch and all were sad about the loss. To a man, they liked the great gaffer who had become a legend in his time. Three straight years a thirty-game winner at Philadelphia, he'd pitched the Phillies to a rare pennant in 1915 and had spun sixteen shutouts in '16 in bandbox Baker Bowl.

That had been with a deader ball. But when the lively whiter ball, changed more frequently, came in with Prohibition, Alex came up with a new pitch. He added a screwball to go with his fast ball and that sharp, short curve, like a later-day slider.

Alexander's forte was incredible control. Once, as a gag, he threw into the mouth of a tomato can moved around the corners of home plate by battermate Bill Killefer. He could pitch with little or no warmup. With the Chicago Cubs, he came out still "under the influence" and used few warmups on a cold day. Working rapidly as was his custom, he shut out his old Philadelphia teammates on one hit—so fast that he was still loaded afterward.

By the time Breadon brought Bill McKechnie back from Rochester in July, sending Southworth back to the International League with the gutsy admission that the boss had been premature in believing Billy was ready, Sam had Alex off taking a "cure" somewhere. Pete came back looking pretty good. He told McKechnie he was wanted to pitch.

The Deacon had his doubts, but Alex shut out the Pirates, presumably tying Christy Mathewson's career record of 372 National League victories. Then a few days later at Philadelphia, the Cardinals tied a game, and McKechnie waved Alex in to relieve.

Bill said, "Hold 'em, Pete, and we'll win this one for you."

Alexander did and the Cardinals did too, in extra innings. They cheered the old fellow in the clubhouse, although there wasn't much to cheer in their first-to-fourth flop from the year before. Apparently the record-breaker with number 373, Old Pete lost all restraint.

McKechnie, who'd been through it with Alexander one too many times, sent the leathery-looking legend back to St. Louis to see Breadon. The clubowner's affection for the hero of the first World Series in 1926 was boundless. He'd never taken a penny in fines from Old Pete. Now, he paid him off for the season in August and told him to go back to Nebraska, to rest up.

Then, someone dredged back through the records and found that Mathewson did indeed have one more victory than previously credited. So Alexander had merely tied Matty, dead for four years, October, 1925. By now, though, in late 1929, time had run out on Alexander, too.

Traded to Philadelphia, Old Pete managed to lose a close one on opening day to the Giants' Carl Hubbell in 1930, 2-1. He never won again. Three defeats and nine appearances later, the forty-three-year-old wandering wonder was released.

The Cardinals, meanwhile, got a good shortstop, Lafayette College's Charley Gelbert, out of the fourth-place (78-74) finish in 1929. Frisch thought Gelbert would have been the best ever if he hadn't been hurt a couple of seasons later.

Grin and Bear It: *Charley Gelbert (right) suffered a badly shot up leg in a hunting accident a year before this 1934 photo. It ruined his brilliant career as a shortstop. He's shown with Bill Walker, lefthanded pitcher out with a broken bone briefly in 1934.*

The Cardinals got still another manager.

For once, Breadon didn't fire his field foreman. But with Singin' Sam's track record for canning 'em, you couldn't blame McKechnie for going to Breadon with the security of a five-year contract from the Boston Braves.

McKechnie's departure from Sportsman's Park paved the way for the coach, Street. Droll, drawling, pipe-puffing Gabby Street, the former batterymate of the great Walter Johnson, was best known as the man who caught a ball dropped off the Washington Monument. He hadn't succeeded in the impossible, i.e., nursemaid to Alexander, but he'd delighted all with his stories of World War I. They called him the Old Sarge.

The yarn-spinning veteran, inheriting a ball club with such future big league managers as Frisch, Wilson, and Bottomley, found his brain trust increased by one at the trading deadline. *The St. Louis Times'* eager-beaver young baseball writer, Sam Muchnick, had been badgering Breadon to deal for the well-traveled pitching greybeard, Burleigh Grimes.

Finally, June 15, as Muchnick and other writers sampled Breadon's hospitality on the road, one Sam brought up the old refrain to the other. Breadon excused himself, went into the hotel bedroom and came out a few minutes later, smiling.

"All right, Sammy, you've got your wish. We just dealt Sherdel and Frankhouse to Boston for Grimes," he said.

Breadon found himself staring at half-empty glasses of bootleg booze as Muchnick and the rest of the press beat it to their typewriters or telephones.

Frisch heard the news with mixed emotions.

"Well, at least I won't have to face that crusty old so-and-so. Crissake, he rounded the edges off my square head. Only time I was ever scared in my life was when that blankety-blank buzzard threw at me on '3 and 0'," he said.

Said Grimes, dryly, after becoming Frisch's roommate and fast friend, "It wasn't '3 and 0.' It was '3 and 1.'"

Even though the Cardinals in mid-August were only fourth with a 53-52 record, twelve games behind the league-leading Brooklyn Robins, Breadon felt good about the future. He surprised everyone by rehiring Street for '31.

At that picnic at Singin' Sam's place, the temperature topped 100 for the seventh time that summer. The Census Bureau announced a 16.1 per cent increase in the United States population from 1920. You could get a two-pants suit for $25 and two diamond rings for $16.85. Fifty cents down, and fifty cents a week—if you had a half buck. The stock market that had collapsed on the Black Tuesday of 1929 had dropped another five to seventeen points.

With Street on hand to umpire a "ball game" between imbibing writers, Breadon raised his glass in toast to the visiting press.

"I wish you'd been here last week when we took four out of five from Brooklyn," he said. "Right now, we're playing the best ball in the league. Too bad we had such a bad start, or I'd have you fellows out here for a World Series . . . "

Ah, ye of little faith! Breadon's Cardinals, perhaps buoyed up putting the skids under Brooklyn, and the announcement that Gabby Street would be back the next year, strung together victories that, coupled with a Dodgers' losing streak, put the defending National League champion Chicago Cubs into first place.

AT THE end of August, exhilarated by a nine-game winning streak, the Redbirds were bobbin' along. They had closed the gap. If only they could win the Series before packed houses at Wrigley Field!

The first game was one for the book. It went twenty innings. In the fifteenth, Bottomley made a brilliant defensive play to prevent the winning run. In extremely long relief, blond Syl Johnson turned back Chicago for twelve innings. In the twentieth, Handy Andy High blooped a run-scoring single. The final score was 8-7, St. Louis.

The next afternoon the Cardinals held a five-run lead into the ninth.

That would be eleven victories in a row, but . . . wait! . . . the Cubs scored five to tie. In the top of the eleventh, Bottomley belted a three-run homer. So now the Cards had 'em for sure, but, no, the Cubbies rebounded again to tie once more. And then, breaking St. Louis' winning streak, grinding that momentum to an apparent halt, Chicago won in the thirteenth, 9-8.

It looked as if the Birds' bid had fallen as flat as the public pocketbook because the Cubs simply murdered St. Louis in the final game of the series, 16-4. Animated fireplug, Hack Wilson, enroute to a league record of fifty-six homers and the astonishing major league standard of 190 RBIs, slugged homers number forty-five and forty-six.

Into September, then, the standings read like this at the top:

Club	W.	L.	Behind
Chicago	77	50	—
New York	70	54	5½
Brooklyn	71	58	7
St. Louis	70	58	7½

But Gabby's guys didn't have sense enough to quit. The Streets picked themselves up and came at the lead again. Now, it was Chicago that faltered. So by mid-September when the Cardinals moved into Ebbets Field, the Dodgers were out in front by only a game over St. Louis. And the Cubs, playing across the bridge at New York, trailed by just a length and a half.

This was, obviously, an era when the ball quivered like a jack rabbit, and the pitchers quavered like quail.

The Cardinals became the only National League club to score 1,000 runs (1004). But in the showdown, pitching will prevail as always. The story takes more twists than a cruller.

For the pivotal series opener, Flint Rhem was scheduled to face the Dodgers' great righthander, Dazzy Vance, the only regular pitcher in the league that year with an earned-run average under 3.00. Then a funny thing happened to Rhem on the way to the key assignment.

So help the old plantation down there at Rhems, South Carolina, "Shad", as the farm boy was known, simply didn't show up. When he arrived, disheveled, he had a terrible story. He'd been standing outside the Cardinals' hotel in New York, he said, minding his own business, when a car drove up. Guys jumped out, pointing a gun at his head. They'd driven him to a hideaway in New Jersey, said Rhem, and forced him to drink raw whiskey. For shame!

Old Shad's "kidnapping" tale sounded as fishy as the tail of any catch he'd taken out of his favorite creek back home. Gabby Street had heard better. Sure, from Rhem. There was a time, for instance, when Flint reeled into the hotel after a night on the town.

"I confess I drank too much," he explained. "But I did it because I figured Old Pete [Alexander] was more valuable to the club. So I tried to drink as much of his share as possible."

When Rhem poured out his yarn about the conspiracy against him and the Cardinals in 1930, it made good writing and reading. At a reunion some years later, Old Shad confessed that the kidnapping story had been for the lower-case birds.

Fortunately, in 1930, Wild Bill Hallahan, although a finger on his right hand was caught in a taxicab door when Ray Blades slammed it, fought back the discomfort. More important, he pitched with his left hand. Hallahan took Rhem's assignment, hooking up with Vance in a dandy duel, a low-scoring honey.

It was scoreless into the tenth when, with Charley Gelbert limping, Andy High batted for the young shortstop against the flame-throwing Vance. Dazzy buzzed two fastballs past the little lefthanded hitter, then threw that overhanded curve. Too high for him, but not for High. Handy Andy rapped it off the fence in right-center for a double. He scored on a base hit by Taylor Douthit.

The Cardinals led. But Brooklyn filled the bases against the makeshift St. Louis lineup with one out in the last of the tenth. The Dodgers' catcher, Al Lopez, rapped a sharp grounder to Earl (Sparky) Adams, shifted to shortstop. The ball bad-hopped, and Sparky juggled it. Then, still not in control, he shoveled the ball to Frank Frisch on the pivot.

"To this day," Lopez moaned of the low spot of his playing career, "I don't think Frisch touched the ball, but merely guided it around to Bottomley. That's how fast Frisch worked to double me."

So the 1-0 masterpiece went to Hallahan and the Cardinals, tying the race. The next day, again with High delivering a pinch double, the Cardinals came from behind to beat wily Cuban righthander Adolph Luque, 5-3. They took first place. And when Grimes outpitched Ray Phelps in the final, 5-3, the Cardinals had swept the series and were in front—to stay.

At the finish, winning thirty-nine of their last forty-nine games for a blistering .796 pace, the Cardinals owned a 92-62 record, a two-length lead over Chicago. There, William Wrigley fired Joe McCarthy the last week of the season. He named Rogers Hornsby as manager.

Frisch congratulated Street for winning 21 of 25 in September. "You're the new miracle man of baseball, Gabby."

"Forget that miracle man stuff, Frank," said the manager to his captain.

"Forget it, nothing," shot back the Flash. "How can you? You'll go down in baseball history that way, like George Stallings and his Miracle Braves in 1914."

The pennant-winning pitching staff was led with fifteen victories by Hallahan, although four others were in double figures; Grimes, Jesse Haines, Flint Rhem and Syl Johnson. Grimes would recall what owner

Wild Bill and the Dazzler: *Above, Bill Hallahan poses with Arthur (Dazzy) Vance at Brooklyn's Ebbets Field before nipping Vance in a 10-inning 1-0 thriller, a pitcher's delight, in 1930.*

Handy Andy: *Left, Little Andy High's timely hitting was a key to the Cardinals' pennant success in the 1930 and '31 world championship. Note his pint-sized glove.*

Sam Breadon had said in mid-June when Grimes had come to the Cardinals.

"If you could just win ten games, Burleigh, we might have a chance . . . "

Grimes was 10 and 1 for the ball club that used its bench magnificently. Batting .314 as a team, they must have seemed as if it were swinging the planks at the plate.

Only the Ball Hawk, the nickname for square-jawed Taylor Douthit in center field, played the entire schedule, batting .303. Gelbert, the great twenty-four-year-old shortstop, played the next most games, 139, and batted a point higher.

Averages were outrageously high. Veteran Ray Blades, used mainly to pinch-hit, batted .396. George (Showboat) Fisher who played part-time outfield defensively as if first bounce were out, hit .374, but was gone the next season. George (Watty) Watkins, the steely-eyed, lean right fielder who looked like a Texas ranger, hit .373.

Young Gus Mancuso, backup catcher to Jimmy Wilson, hit .366 as a rookie, far higher than seasons thereafter. Another part-timer, Ernie Orsatti, finished with .321. Among regulars, Sparky Adams, the leadoff man at third base, batted .314, four points fewer than mitt-and-mask man Wilson. Bottomley, at first base, hit .304.

The leaders, all-round, in the judgment of the annual Spalding Guide, forerunner of the annual Spink Baseball Guide, were Frisch and Hafey. The Flash drove in 114 runs with his .346 average, playing 133 games. Hafey, although limited to 120 by his visual problem, drove in 107 when hitting twenty-six homers and batting .336.

Andy High, handier than his .279 average would indicate, could chide Frisch with admiration about his "convenient lumbago," a condition that annually almost seemed to grab the Flash with muscle spasms in his lower back.

"Ace Wilson used to say, 'Better take some ground balls at second base, Andy, I think the Flash is going to take his summer 'vacation,'" said High, smiling.

"Sure enough, Frank would be out in the dog days of August, get rested up and then return, refreshed. And when he smelled the World Series' lettuce, he was a whirling dervish. You couldn't beat him. Or, as Lou Gehrig said, if you got Frisch mad, he'd beat you by himself."

That's about the way Nick Altrock, clownish Washington coach and former great American League lefthander, saw it in a syndicated Series preview in which, picking the Philadelphia Athletics to whip the Cardinals in five games as they had the Cubs in 1929, he wrote:

"Frankie Frisch of the Cards is the kind of money player that would bust a ligament playing second base if the Series winners only got derby hats.

"In the last ten years there has hardly been a World Series when Frisch hasn't been in the lineup. If a season finished without Frankie copping some extra Series cash, he wouldn't know whether to take the poor debtor's oath or to have a nervous breakdown . . .

"But I still stick by my heavy artillery; Lefty Grove and George Earnshaw. The rest of Connie Mack's pitching staff still looks like the upper half of a pinochle deck. If the Cards expect to beat that layout, they will have to play backgammon . . . "

In the year of the most hitting ever, pitching prevailed in the Series, the Cardinals batting just .200 and Philadelphia a mere .197. But the Athletics out long-balled the Redbirds. Off Grimes, for instance, in the opener, the world champions got only five hits. All were for extra bases, including homers by Mickey Cochrane and Al Simmons. They won, 5-2, behind the great Grove, their 28-and-5 overpowering lefthander.

Cochrane also homered as Moose Earnshaw beat Rhem, 6-1. Then, returning to St. Louis, the Cardinals evened the Series. Hallahan shut out southpaw rival Rube Walberg, 5-0. Pop Haines, for whom Branch

Best Bet for a Laugh: Hat typically twisted sideways, former Chicago American League pitching star, Nick Altrock, was a Washington coaching-lines' comedian whose essays showed that he thought Frank Frisch was not funny to the foe.

Rickey had borrowed $10,000 to buy from Kansas City in 1920, out-pitched Grove, 3-1.

So, the next day, the Series really hung in the balance when Grimes dueled scorelessly with Earnshaw, who left for a pinch-hitter in the eighth inning. Grove, none other, was the Moose's replacement into the ninth.

Cochrane, first up, walked, and Burleigh faced Simmons, the long-sleeved regular-season .381 slugger who had batted in 165 runs. Grimes got him. The excited St. Louis crowd sighed. Too soon.

Up came bulging-biceped Jimmy Foxx, the bronzed home-run hitter. Once, in the first game of the Series, Grimes had fooled Foxxie with a curve ball when logic was that Old Stubblebeard would throw his money pitch, the quick-dipping sinker. Now, Burleigh tried to curve again, but, alas, the muscular Double-X was thinking along with him.

The home run Foxx hit was a majestic blow, high and deep into the left-center bleachers.

Meanwhile, a Missouri judge, hurrying with friends for a return automobile trip to Kansas City, was asked the score at a gas station.

"Jimmy Foxx two, Cardinals nothing," said the bespectacled jurist, a man named Harry S Truman.

Back in Philadelphia, the Athletics got only seven hits two days later. All were for extra bases, including a double and home run by third baseman Jimmy Dykes, and a homer by Simmons. Hallahan had retired early, ineffective with a blister on his pitching hand. Earnshaw, with a sparkling 0.72 earned-run average for the Series, breezed by a 7-1 score.

The Cardinals faced a long train trip back to St. Louis. The $3,536.68 loser's share would go a lot further in bad times than the $4,181.30 Frisch, and others had received in the good ol' last gasp days of the Fat-Cat '20s two years earlier.

Strapped with tape because of a lumbago seizure that had dropped him to his knees next to his hotel bed the morning of the first Series game, Frisch had been under the tender care of trainer Harrison J. (Doc) Weaver. Good old Bucko and Frankie's fast friend, Dr. Robert F. Hyland, the club surgeon, had tried so hard, but Frisch had had a miserable Series, batting just .208, committing three errors.

Although Frisch silently moaned to himself in sorrow and self-pity, he growled aloud when he heard a melodic chant from the back of the bus.

"It's all over now . . . it's all over now . . . ''

Grimes, another hard loser, heard it too. Burleigh got up and walked back to where a strapping young outfielder, big George Puccinelli, sat sing-songing.

"It's all over now . . . it's . . . . . ''

"Listen, you big S.O.B.," snapped Grimes, "we know it's all over, but, dammit, we don't want to hear about it."

In sixteen times at bat with the Cardinals at the end of the 1930 season, George Puccinelli had batted a blazing .563 with nine hits, including a double and three home runs. But, in 1931, Pooch didn't wear the uniform with the trademark of the Redbirds rampant on a bat.

The Salty Pepper: Strong-armed, awkward, enthusiastic Pepper Martin used to sling his bat often. One day, the bat slipped into the dugout next to the Cardinals and struck the wife of the Cardinals' clubowner, Mrs. Sam Breadon.

11
The Wild Horse
Trumps an Ace

THE wide-shouldered, hawk-nosed man with the bronzed features of an Indian and the brashness of his also-Irish ancestry burst into Branch Rickey's office early in the 1931 season. In the nasal twang of the Southwest, the Wild Horse of the Osage was an agitated Oklahoman the way anyone rarely saw him.

Johnny Leonard Roosevelt (Pepper) Martin was angry.

"John Brown," he said, using the proper name to substitute for an expletive the way the general manager employed Judas Priest, "if you can't play me, Mr. Rickey, trade me."

Pepper had a point. Besides, B.R. liked him because he was a God-fearing, Bible-quoting imitation of Rickey himself. Over the years, he would become evangelistic and oratorical even if he didn't always use the polysyllabics in the right place.

At twenty-seven, Martin, an outfielder, hadn't even a major league demitasse in the way of a trial, pinch-running here and there and rarely getting in to a ball game. He was awkward, but aggressive, strong as a sawed-off Paul Bunyan.

Rickey had considerably more compassion for Pepper than he did for that skinny righthander, Dizzy Dean. Diz had come up from Houston at the end of the Texas League season in 1930. When the Cardinals clinched that come-from-behind pennant the final weekend, manager Gabby Street named him to pitch the last game of the season.

As the lanky, long-legged lad, just nineteen, warmed up in front of the third-base dugout, St. Louis mayor Victor Miller called Street over to congratulate him. He also asked Street what he thought of Dizzy.

"Mr. Mayor," drawled the Old Sarge in beardless prophecy, "I believe he's going to be a great pitcher, but I'm afraid we're not going to know from one minute to the next what he's going to do."

Early in the 1930 season, bought out of the regular Army by Pa Dean, Dizzy had signed with the Cardinals and had been assigned to St. Joseph, Missouri, the Western League farm club. In St. Joe, the breezy big galoot had won big and lived the same way. He'd rented rooms simultaneously in three hotels.

At Houston, he'd won eight out of ten decisions to give him 25-and-10. One night coming in late, he encountered Fred Ankenman, president of the Houston ball club. Dizzy was big about it.

"Looks as if we's both a little late, Mr. President," said the Great One, who said he'd gone only to fourth grade in school because he didn't want to pass his Pappy. "If you won't say nuthin' to anybody about seein' me, I won't say nuthin' about seein' you."

In spring training, 1931, at Bradenton, Florida, Dean was a pain in the baggy-flannel baseball britches to Street, and to Rickey and to club-owner Sam Breadon.

Dizzy had the urge to splurge. Finally, Clarence Lloyd, the traveling secretary, was ordered to tell the Bradenton businessmen to advance no credit to the man-child. Dean was put on a dollar-a-day allowance. That rule held, even the one day when he'd skipped picking up his George Washington's picture, and he was crushed to learn that he couldn't have $2 the next day.

Dean was seen and heard. That is, when he didn't oversleep like a growing boy. He crowed that given a regular starting turn, he'd win thirty games. Street tried to put him in his place by pitching him an inning against the world champion Athletics, but Dizzy had the last laugh and last word.

In succession, Ol' Diz, as he referred to himself before he had touched twenty, struck out Mickey Cochrane, Al Simmons and Jimmy Foxx. He told Street, and all who'd listen, "Criminy, if you guys had had me last fall, you'd a won from those fellas."

Finally, when a frustrated Street was certain Dizzy needed a lesson, he recommended that Dean be optioned out. Rickey called Dizzy in to tell the Great One he'd been returned to the Texas League. Big blond Jim Lindsey, the relief pitcher, smiled and brought forth a clubhouse chuckle when he said, "So help me, the fastest I ever saw a club lose thirty games."

But, of course, the 1931 Cardinals were a set ball club, the best of eight championship teams on which Frank Frisch said he'd ever played. There was such job competition that Pepper Martin, that Leap Year baby born just before the St. Louis World's Fair opened in '04, wondered, John Brown, what a guy had to do to get a chance to play before he tripped over his own beard?

Now, if there was one thing Branch Rickey prided himself in, other than in cutting corners to make more money for Sam Breadon and himself, it was the ability to watch a player and see just a little too soon, rather than too late, that the athlete had gone over the hill.

The center fielder, Taylor Douthit, was an outstanding defensive player and a good enough hitter. But B.R. noticed something. The Ball Hawk seemed to have lost a step. He was swinging a bit late on the ball. Besides, why pay a ball player $14,500 when you can get one for $4,500?

Rickey, generally believed the highest-salaried executive next to $65,000-a-year commissioner Judge Landis, was a lawyer, ball player, football coach, manager, bridge expert and anything else that smacked of the smarts. But he dressed as if he slept in his rumpled suits. And so did the protege whose "sense of adventure" he admired—Johnny Martin.

When a coat and necktie were absolute, hairy-chested Pepper would go around in his shirt sleeves, open at the collar, wearing a five-gallon hat tilted back on his high forehead. He carried a theatrical trunk on the road, but like the pickup truck he drove, it wasn't for clothes. Instead, it carried shotguns, farm equipment, machinery parts, and other knick-knacks that appealed to Pepper.

OVER THE years, despite that relatively late start as a regular, the Wild Horse became a legend, one to be dealt with at greater length when the Cardinals officially became the Gas House Gang. To deal with the Gang without emphasizing Pepper Martin and Dizzy Dean would be like talking of Abbott without Costello, or Laurel without Hardy.

For Pep, the legend began when Rickey dealt Douthit to Cincinnati at the trading deadline in 1931. "Tay," a smart player, read voraciously, and he smelled a trade. He didn't want to leave the ball club for which he'd played on three pennant winners. The weekend of June 15, boosting his 1931 average to .336 Douthit was never better, ripping eight hits in nine trips.

That should stop the trade talk, he thought. Alas, the deed had already been done, consummated on a Friday and to be announced on a Monday because of a technicality.

Meanwhile, Martin hit an even .300 in 1931, the year in which the sacrifice fly was stricken from the scoring rules, and the ball was deadened a bit to cut averages so that clubowners could feel comfortable in cutting salaries. The individual league leader was more than fifty points behind Bill Terry's 1930 .401, the last over .400 in the NL.

The Cardinals' Hafey won the batting championship in '31. Chick had a fractional point over Terry and St. Louis teammate Jim Bottomley, both of whom hit .348. Even Frisch dipped to .311, but was still voted Most Valuable Player.

The National League, like the American, had dropped the official award for the champ. The Baseball Writers Association of America picked it up and continued to sponsor it—but without the $1000 bag of gold. Frank got the award, but only a trophy.

Frisch could be good, and fresh, all right, as Art Devlin had told John McGraw before the Giants scouted him in 1919. Once, he'd come up swinging against the scrappy infielder, Jimmy Smith, Billy Conn's father-in-law, later credited with having decked the light heavyweight champion. Another time, the Flash bunted safely against Bill Doak, the man for whom Rawlings Sporting Goods made the most famous of all baseball gloves. The Flash stood at first base and thumbed his nose.

But the bubbling personality and good humor that, although it could be cutting sarcasm and ridicule at times, yet never vicious, emerged more, and more.

In '31 during an early June of a thirteen and a half game pennant runaway, the Redbirds were playing a get-away game on Ladies' Day. As a Depression gimmick, the Cardinals would open their gates to the fair sex one day a week. With Thomas Patrick (Convey) beating the airways like an early-day Harry Caray or Jack Buck, the women would fling down their scrub buckets and hand-cranked washing machines for a fifty cents' service charge admission.

That day, a good crowd saw the Philly's Klein hammer a first inning home run off Grimes. Into the ninth, righthanded Ray Benge held that 1-0 lead. Burleigh boiled as he left the lineup for a last inning pinch-hitter. He stormed into the clubhouse and proceeded to dismantle the place.

With two outs, Watty Watkins suddenly homered, tying the score. On the next pitch, with the women guests still on their feet cheering Watkins, Frisch lofted a high fly just fair and inside the foul line, onto the right field roof for a 310-foot home run that won the unusual game, 2-1.

Laughing at the startled, then beaming Grimes, the Cardinals rushed by cabs to catch a train headed East at the Bremen Avenue station. And the St. Louis Star's Walter W. Smith, who would win a national reputation from New York as syndicated humorist Red Smith, referred to the Flash's blow as "the longest home run in history because Frisch talked about it all the way from St. Louis to Boston."

The 1931 race was a piece of cake for the Cardinals, who had a 101-53 record. The A's cadillacked to a third straight pennant in the American League with 107 victories.

In a last-day field meet designed to aid the boxoffice of a runaway, ho-hum race, the Redbirds played Brooklyn. One of the events was a 75-

yard dash for a $100 cash prize. Young speedsters Pepper Martin and Ernie Orsatti were favored, but jumping the gun like a quick accelerating base-stealer, Frankie Frisch leaped into the lead, and held on to win, his cap popping off to reveal the bald pate of an athlete who was thirty-four that month, and wise in the head.

Before the World Series, Stockton suggested that Martin, the unknown rookie, just might be the Series hero. Overnight, Pepper became a household word.

From the time he faced Lefty Grove, an astonishing 31-and-4 pitcher that year, with two on and two out in the first inning, and prayed "God be my helper," Martin was marvelous. His two-run double was wasted because Grove's teammates teed off on twenty-four-year-old rookie Paul Derringer, Gabby Street's gambling choice over the experienced Hallahan and Grimes. The score was 6-2.

In the second game, a battle between Hallahan and Earnshaw, Wild Bill won a wild one, 2-0. The offense was all Martin. Pep had two hits, one a double, stole two bases, and scored both runs, one on a squeeze play. The game ended on a wild, controversial note.

Philadelphia had two on, two out in the visitors' ninth when pinch-hitter Jimmy Moore apparently struck out on an overhanded curve ball into the dirt.

Wilson had only to tag out Moore as he turned toward the bench or to peg the ball to Bottomley at first. But, as the baserunners broke, the smart catcher blanked. He threw down to Jake Flowers at third base. Flowers, replacing injured Sparky Adams, was not on the bag. So no force-out was involved.

As the crowd began to pour out of the stands, plate umpire Dick Nallin stood his ground. Eddie Collins, coaching third for the A's, raced down to the plate area. Eddie urged Moore to run to first base, which by then was uncovered.

An argument took time before the field was cleared. Instead of being in the clubhouse with a shutout, Hallahan had to pitch with the bases loaded to Max Bishop, the A's walk-wheedling leadoff man. Would Hallahan be Wild Bill and walk the park? Or Sweet William and get the ball over with good stuff?

Bishop hoisted a foul toward temporary seats behind first base. Bottomley drifted over toward the belt-high barrier with Frisch charging over from second, yelling "Plenty of room, Jim, plenty of room . . . "

Bottomley barged into the wooden barrier, reached backhanded into the crowd to make a brilliant catch. As he trotted off, Frisch gleefully pounded his back.

"What did you mean 'Plenty of room?' " Sunny Jim, shaken up, half-griped.

Frisch grinned. "But you made the catch, Jim, old boy, didn't you?" he said.

In the third game, one in which Martin belted two hits, including a double, and drove in a run off Grove, it was Frisch's turn to play high-wire acrobat. After Grimes held the A's hitless until the eighth inning at Philadelphia, leading 4-0, Jimmy Foxx walked and Bing Miller got the A's first of two hits, a single.

With two on and two out, Roger (Doc) Cramer hit a sharp line drive toward right-center for an apparent two-run double. But Frisch broke rapidly to his left, leaped and speared the ball, tumbling to the ground.

Wilson, the native Philadelphian who almost had been the Series goat with his mental boo-boo, hailed the second baseman's position play as well as his agility.

"Day in and day out, Frank is in there doing baseball stunts that escape the eyes of the fans, but not the players," he said. "He knows how to make the plays at bat and in the field. He shifts for every hitter because he's got a book on them in his brain . . . "

But the 1931 Series was Pepper Martin's, at least for five games during which he rattled twelve hits, including four doubles and a home run. Even though Grove, and Earnshaw stopped him the last two games, the Wild Horse of the Osage ran wild, stealing five bases, scoring five runs, driving in five and batting .500.

So the Redbirds were alive, thanks largely to Martin's magic, and the pitching of Hallahan and Grimes. The Series went to a seventh game. The Cardinals got only five hits, bunched by the top two men in the batting order, Andy High, and Watty Watkins. Between them, with Watkins hitting a two-run homer in the third inning, the Cardinals jumped to an early 4-0 lead.

As the thirty-eight-year-old Grimes came to the bench at the end of the eighth, the Cardinals' old bullpen catcher, Mike Gonzalez sauntered up to the third-base dugout. Presumably he wanted a drink of water.

But as the Cuban explained in his cracked-ice English, "Mike, she no thirsty. She wanna see Burleigh eyes. Ah, Burleigh, eyes tire. So Mike, she go back to bullpen and say, 'Hey Moong . . . '"

"Moong" was the closest Gonzalez could come to "Moon," the round-faced Hallahan's nickname.

"Moong, you get rady. Tomorrow, she open date," he said.

So Hallahan, who had allowed only one run in two starts, was limbering when suddenly with two outs, two A's scored. Street came out, talked to Grimes, turned and summoned Hallahan, who once again faced Bishop in a jam.

This time Max hit the ball sharply to left center, but, appropriately, hero Pepper Martin thundered over and made the Series-ending catch.

In the raucous, Sportsman's Park clubhouse, Judge Landis congratulated Martin.

"Young man," he said, "I'd rather trade places with you than with any man in the country."

The eagle-beaked, wide-shouldered guy with the ear-to-ear grin said, "Why, that'll be just fine, Judge, if we can trade salaries, too."

12

A Lost Voyage for Marco Polo

IF FRANKIE FRISCH had known what lay over the baseball rainbow for him in 1932—a brass gabboon rather than a pot of gold—he probably would have kept going on an ocean trip around the world after a baseball trip to Japan.

Pepper Martin hardly had squeezed that line drive to dethrone the powerful Philadelphia Athletics on a early-October Saturday, when Frisch and three members of the beaten A's were off to meet the rest of their Nippon-bound party waiting on the West Coast.

Accompanied by Lefty Grove, Mickey Cochrane and Al Simmons of the losing team, and with tall, distinguished Frederick G. Lieb, a longtime New York baseball writer, Frisch skeedaddled by train to Kansas City. A little snug plane, the same type on which Notre Dame's Knute Rockne had crashed to death earlier the same year, was scheduled to fly to Los Angeles.

97

Instead, high winds forced them to go by rail to Amarillo, Texas, where they were again told turbulence was too risky. At Albuquerque, New Mexico, they finally were airborne. They were immediately airsick, too, especially Cochrane, who was upset from the humiliation of Pepper Martin's stolen bases and unhappy over heavy losses in the stock-market crash. Frisch needled Black Mike about the embarrassment of Pepper's salty play, aware that neither Grove nor George Earnshaw had done a decent job at keeping the Wild Horse tethered.

Finally, Fred Lieb whispered, "Lay off, Frank. Cochrane is ready to crack up."

The bracing salt-water air of the Pacific aboard a Japanese liner helped take the snap-crackle-and-pop out of Cochrane's nerves. The lineup put together by Lieb and a former marginal major leaguer, Herb Hunter, a promoter who had taken Casey Stengel and others to Japan eight years earlier, was an impressive one.

Lou Gehrig, Frisch, Rabbit Maranville and Willie Kamm were in the infield. Simmons, Tom Oliver and Lefty O'Doul were in the outfield. Cochrane and Muddy Ruel were the catchers. Grove, Larry French and Bruce Cunningham were the pitchers. The utility players were George Kelly and Ralph Shinners.

The players got a free ride, of course, but they had to pay for their wives. Frisch got miffed, Lieb recalled, when Flash learned that Gehrig was getting $5,000 and Simmons, Cochrane and Grove lesser sums. The tour included $500 for forty-year-old Maranville as player-manager.

After a ball-game stop at Honolulu, the All-Stars swept a seventeen-game series from Japan's top teams, which were then college players. The Americans hit .346 as a team, using a Japanese-made ball that was livelier than the U.S. product. They outscored their hosts 129 to 30.

The sponsoring newspaper, Yoniuri Shimbun, had promised an ornate silver jewel case to the tour's top hitter. The old money player, Frisch, might have won it, hitting .444, but O'Doul, the gifted batting Brooklyn outfielder who began a life-long love affair with the Japanese, found one English-speaking little second baseman he didn't like.

"O'Doodle," the big San Franciscan in a traditional green Irish suit, dragged a bunt to get the source of his annoyance to cover first base. But the Jap was quicker with his hip than Lefty. He hipped O'Doul up in the air and out of action so that his early-tour average stayed at a prize-winning .615.

Among the Japanese, the American favorites were the five-foot-five pixie, Maranville, who marched one day in one of their military parades, and the towering (six-foot-three) Grove, who threw so blasted hard.

To a man, amused by the proliferation of bicycles from Tokyo to Sendai, Osaka to Yokohama, the big leaguers were convinced in their nine-city stop that (1) the Japanese were as baseball batty and as militaristic as their invasion of Manchuria indicated, and (2) that the future of baseball lay in professional teams, not in college ball.

"Actually," Frisch observed through an interpreter, "you field better than American college players. You make fewer mistakes, especially throwing errors, when we put running pressure on you. You don't have the size to have the same power of a Gehrig or Simmons, but you need heavier bats, and to swing them, not just chop or push at the ball."

The tour of Japan didn't end until November 30. As the rest of the American baseball tourists headed back for the West Coast, Frisch said to heck with the cheapskates, just as he had railed at American umpire John (Beans) Reardon. The New England Irishman missed what the Flash thought was an inning-ending third strike when Frisch pitched a couple of innings of a runaway game, giving up a run.

"Crissake, Beans," Frisch beefed, just as he would many times on a hot ball field or over a cold beer, "I had a man struck out. I thought you missed 'em in the Occident by accident, but you're just as lousy in the Orient."

With his passage paid back to New York, Frisch added to it. He took Ada on a Dollar Line luxury ship, the President Harrison. Stops were made at Kobe, Shanghai, Hong Kong, Manila, Singapore, Penang, Ceylon, and through the Suez Canal on an eleven-day cruise to Cairo, followed by Alexandria, Naples, Vesuvius, Rome, Pompeii, Genoa, Marseilles and . . . .

Back at the New York Athletic Club, Frisch sank in a deep leather chair and gave his litany to the New York Times' John Kieran. Frank politely omitted the silks and other treasure troves he and Ada had brought back for their new English-style home out on New Rochelle's Fenimore Road, just forty-five minutes from Broadway.

He talked about meeting Fordham priests at Manila, of taking home movies, riding camels in Egypt, and meeting French salts of the Seven Seas drying out fish nets on the Old Fort at Marseilles. Fishing smacks at anchor in the sparkling harbor of the wide, blue Mediterranean made a lasting impression on "Marco Polo," as Kieran called the globe-girdler who had been gone until the New Year was no thumb-sucking infant.

As always, though, Frisch drooled about eating, comparing the President Harrison's cuisine with the festive board of the S.S. Levithan, on which he and Ada had gone to England with the Giants in the fall of 1924.

Of course, he took tea in Ceylon, said the Flash, sounding like a sophisticated line out of a Cole Porter lyric.

"Went through one of the Lipton plantations and packing houses," he added. "And, oh, boy, was it hot down there! Say, talk about tea—we had it every afternoon on deck when we were aboard ship. Six meals a deal! What a life for a fellow who's supposed to be an athlete!"

"Yeah, breakfast when you got up, bouillon at eleven, then lunch, tea at five, dinner at seven, and sandwiches and coffee before going to bed."

The whirling-dervish Flash of 1927, the year he'd trimmed from 170 to

165 before spring training, then had melted in his dazzling season to 151, had ballooned on his world cruise to 185.

Hadn't he exercised?

"Oh, I managed to get in a little," Frisch told Kieran. "One of the mates on board had played ball, so when he was off watch in the daytime, we used to go on the top deck forward, and pitch and catch in our bathing suits an hour or so."

Arm, yes, but legs no. The weight had come down unnaturally, too. Once the good ship President Harrison passed Gibraltar and emerged into the wintry Atlantic, snow, wind, and waves—"stahm aftuh stahm" as Frisch put it—caused the Flash to flash his hash with a turnaround case of *mal de mer*. Now, he hurried off to a handball court. Too late.

At a victory party in St. Louis immediately after the 1931 Series, when Frisch was headed Far East, Branch Rickey had furrowed his brow and grumbled, "Great day and season, indeed, but I keep wondering what are we going to do when Frisch finishes?"

This, mind you, from the man whose farm system was now turning out talent like an automobile assembly line in Detroit.

Frisch had hit only .259 in the '31 Series, but, as mentioned, he'd won the National League's coveted Most Valuable Player award, prompting Hearst's crack New York columnist, Bill Corum, to comment.

"There's life in the old Bronx boy yet. Until a better second baseman comes leaping out of the bushes with his hair in a braid, Frank the Fordham can go on patrolling the middle for my scratch.

"It was especially pleasing to see him get this award at this time since, so far as playing honors go, it just about leaves him with the lot. Years hence, as he sits by the fireside wooing the echo of half-forgotten cheers, he can say:

" 'And in 1931, thirteen years after I started and after seven World Series, they still called me the Most Valuable Player in my league.'

"It's been a long time, as the years skim by, since Frisch was the Pepper Martin of a World Series, a capless horseman of our Giants running riot over and around and through the startled, stolid Yankees. Frankie no longer runs from under his cap. He seldom tries that old headlong dive. His hair is edging back off the forehead and there is a round bald spot visible on top when he uncovers for the strains of 'The Star Spangled Banner.' His waist has thickened and now and again, especially in the spring, he catches the misery in his legs and back. But as I remarked, he still can pack his weight on the field when the chips are down.

" . . . In the old days his dazzling speed made up for the two or three extra motions he managed to work into a [double] play. But I noticed during the Series that where once he beat 'em by a step, he now is missing some of them by the same margin."

Corum thought Frisch had missed what he called a Sears-and-Roebuck double play, "made to order," that deprived Burleigh Grimes of a shutout in the '31 Series. And horse-playing Broadway Bill reverted to race-track parlance with a sobering sum-up.

"That's the tell, as we say at the club. They look just the same out there, but they're missing 'em. When that starts happening regularly, it won't be long . . ."

Frisch, dropping off in 1932 to .292, his first time under .300 since his first full season in the majors back in 1920, had only one of his 115 games in which he resembled the devastating Flash of old, not an old Flash. On Tuberculosis Day, always a special St. Louis occasion that drew well on a weekday, the old ham at second base responded to the hoopla. Righthanded, he clubbed one home run onto the right field roof, another into the right-center field pavilion. He also singled.

But he didn't cover the ground with those gasping plays as of before. And painfully to admirers, as well as caustically to critics, he jogged to first base on infield outs rather than to speed down there as when—at times—he had even slid headfirst into the bag.

Frisch, maintained by at least two of his literary admirers, Sid Keener and Ray Gillespie, appeared to be "laying down."

Roy Stockton, another friend, decided to put it to him personally one day in Pittsburgh's Schenley Hotel.

"Frank," said Stockton, "they're saying tough things about you, that you're not trying all-out, that you're trying to get Gabby Street's job."

Frisch's sleepy eyes widened, then flashed angrily. That nasal, high-pitched voice raised an octave.

"Hasn't the old S.O.B. told you what's wrong with me?" said Frisch. Stockton shook his head.

"Come up to my room," requested the Flash.

Upstairs, Frisch unbuckled his trousers and dropped them to his ankles, displaying thighs taped from hips to knees.

"Dammit, Roy," he said, "I'm playing on the worst possible char-leyhorses because, even under par, I'm better than anyone else Gabby can put out there."

Frisch paused, hiking his pants.

"No," he said, "I'm not looking for the alibiing old such-and-such's job. But, I'll tell you this, if I ever DO manage a ball club and I have to use a man under par, I'll let the press know." (He did.)

To Stockton, the foldup of the world champions wasn't unexpected. In spring training, the experienced eye and alert ears of the veteran baseball writer had seen and heard. He knew that some of the champions were living it up at beach cottages. He knew, too, that, suddenly, good ol' Gabby Street had decided to become expert.

STREET WAS tired of reading about that great brain trust, he said, without mentioning Frisch or Jim Wilson or Jim Bottomley or Chick Hafey or Jesse Haines or the one who had been traded, Burleigh

Changing of the Guard: *Shortly before Frank Frisch succeeded Gabby Street as manager in July, 1933, the once good friends huddled, obviously reserved in their feelings. Typically, the Flash's hat sits high, flat-topped.*

Grimes. He'd do the thinking from now on. So stow the suggestions. Understand?

They understood, all right, better than they understood the Cardinals' management. Sure, times were tough. For instance, that 623,960 attendance in 1931 had been bettered three times in the five previous years. But did Breadon and Rickey have to unload higher-salaried players without return?

Grimes, the gallant big-game gaffer getting about $20,000, had been dealt to Chicago for another high-paid guy, Hack Wilson, the Peck's Bad Boy slugger who had dipped alarmingly in one season. Rickey must have known Hack wouldn't buy that proposed salary reduction from nearly $40,000 to $7,500.

"Hell, Mr. Rickey, that ain't a salary cut, that an amputation," said Wilson. Quickly he was sold by the Cardinals to Brooklyn for $40,000 and a warm body. Hack never put on a St. Louis uniform.

The Hafey case was pathetic. After the 1927 season, Chick had signed a three-year contract that called for $8,000, $9,000 and $10,000. Even though playing no more that 138 games any season, he'd batted .337, .338 and .336, belted twenty-seven, twenty-nine and twenty-six homers, and knocked in 111, 125 and 107 runs. Consistency, thy name was Chick. John McGraw had said the fleet, powerful-throwing outfielder, with two good eyes, would be the best player in baseball.

Contracts weren't renegotiated then. So Chick was stuck. Then when his chance came, the Depression had given management an excuse. Hafey wanted $15,000. Finally, Breadon and Rickey gave it to him, but not until opening day. Then they blithely sent the holdout to Danville, Illinois, to get in shape, docking his pay $2,100 until they deemed he was ready. So for leading the league in 1931 with .349, Chick got $12,900.

Now, he wanted $15,000 and the return of that money they'd taken from him. Rickey invited him to Florida. Chick motored from his California home, found the front office unbending, and drove furiously back, coast to coast.

They waited until opening day again. This time they exiled Hafey to Cincinnati, then the Siberia of the National League, getting two undistinguished players and an unannounced amount of their favorite commodity: cash.

Any wonder morale was lower than the Cardinals' finish? The tie for sixth and seventh was the farthest a world championship ball club ever fell in one season.

Outfielders Ernie Orsatti and Watty Watkins did well enough, but World Series hero Pepper Martin skidded to .238, and, well, a team batting average dip to .269 told much of the story. Not only Marco Polo Frisch, the world traveler, flopped in the Flash's most unforgettably forgettable season.

An exception was that rawboned righthander who had come up the final day of the season two years ago, beat Pittsburgh on a three-hitter, 3-1, but then talked himself back in to a return trip to Houston. There, Dizzy Dean found twenty-six victories and a wife, a Mississippi miss named Patricia Nash. She wouldn't marry him at home plate, but she shrewdly began to see to it that Ol' Diz didn't give away his good fortune. He made $3,000 that year and—try this on your budget!—Pat saved $1,200 of it.

But now, in his first season in the majors, working his skinny tail off for a Redbird with droopy tail feathers, he put together an 18-15 season. And one day against the Giants in June, he bunted what amounted to a home run.

Actually, it went this way:

With the New York third baseman charging, Dizzy popped the bunt over the Giant's head into short left field and hightailed into second. When the throw-in sailed past the second baseman, Dean lit out for third. When Mel Ott's throw from right skimmed past third, an exhausted Dizzy spiked home plate.

The next day, John J. McGraw quit as manager of the Giants. After thirty years, he'd seen quite enough.

The Lip: *Slick, brassy Leo Durocher was the good-field, no-hit shortstop for whom the Cardinals gave up a good pitcher, Paul Derringer, early in 1933 to shore up the sag in their infield.*

13
Lippy Comes, Gabby Goes

THE SLIM fashion plate with the slicked-back hair and booming voice burst into Branch Rickey's office, unannounced, uninvited and did the unexpected. He began by calling the Mahatma by his first name, which even Mrs. Rickey rarely did in public.

"Branch," roared Leo Durocher, freshly acquired from Cincinnati, "I'm glad to be aboard and I'll help you win pennants, but if you think I'm going to do it for a measly $6,000 a year . . . "

Taken aback, bemused and then amused at the brashness of Lippy Leo, Rickey let Durocher make his sideshow barker's pitch for a salary increase, then finally cleared his throat, and began.

"Listen, young man, I've seen your contract. It's already got more stapled-in clauses caused by debt than that free spender in the White House [Franklin D. Roosevelt]. You straighten out your own affairs

105

before you tell ME how to run MINE, and, by the way, YOU show ME just how good you are, and we'll talk. Now, goodbye."

"Okay, Branch," said Durocher, unabashed as when he breezed into the office of the Cardinals' general manager who had traded him for Paul Derringer.

The truth is, the Cardinals were desperate because twenty-six-year-old Charley Gelbert, regarded by Frank Frisch as the best young shortstop he'd ever seen, had almost shot off a foot when he tripped, rabbit hunting in November.

By then, the old guard was beginning to go, and a new clan to gather, the guys who would become known as the Gas House Gang.

Late in the 1932 season, they had brought up from Houston a waddling twenty-year-old outfielder with power in his black bat and quick fists, Joe Medwick. If you want to argue that if the Cardinals hadn't dealt Chick Hafey to the Reds before the '32 season, there wouldn't have been room for Medwick, there IS no rule that says Chick and Ducky-Wucky couldn't have played in the same outfield at the same time. What a 1-2 righthanded thump-thump that would have been!

Hafey's long-time power partner, Sunny Jim Bottomley, had been dealt in December of '32 to—what else—Cincinnati, where Rickey periodically offered Sidney Weil, a nice insurance man, his advice, and sympathy, and, oh, yes, an aging ball player for a cover-up clone of a major leaguer. Naturally, money. Not a lot because of the vanishing dollar, but a little. And, as always, B.R. unloaded a pretty good salary when he sent away the thirty-two-year-old popular Sunny Jim.

Too long at Rochester, the Redbirds had held back a banjo-eyed ample-nosed character named Jimmy (The Ripper) Collins, a switch-hitting first baseman from the Pennsylvania coal country. Collins was probably the best long-ball hitter among turn-around batters until Mickey Mantle. He had come up in '32, played some outfield and relieved Bottomley at first base. He'd hit twenty-one home runs, power production the Cardinals needed.

Why—and this one always seems to surprise just casual followers of baseball—they even reacquired Rogers Hornsby so that, yes, if you're ever asked the trivia question, Hornsby and Frisch did play on the same ball club.

The Rajah had his moments, but a tough time after leaving St. Louis. When the Giants traded him to Boston in 1927, New York finally had got John McGraw's long-awaited box office attraction, a Jewish ball player. Immediately, the New York press had pitted the fast-starting Andy Cohen's in a daily comparison with Hornsby's slow getaway at Braves Field.

On the Braves' first visit to the Polo Grounds, Hornsby told New York writers, "You guys are doing the kid an injustice. I'll leave the poor bleep in the dust."

Cohen, not helped when he was wined and dined by every proud Jewish organization around the National League, dipped down to .274,

Yes, They Did: Frisch greets a long-time rival, Hall of Fame second baseman Rogers Hornsby, two years older at 37, when he came back to the Cards' training camp in 1933.

en route to a shortlived major league career. The Rajah hit .387 to lead the league at Boston. "Yes," Casey Stengel would say with a knowing wink, ".387 against the wind."

Although Hornsby managed much of the season for the embarrassing Braves, whose incredibly poor 50-103 record was only the second-poorest in the league (Philly finished 43-109), clubowner Judge Emil Fuchs didn't want to deal Hornsby when Bill Veeck, Sr. of the Chicago Cubs came calling. General Manager Veeck and Joe McCarthy thought Chicago needed one player for a pennant.

"Judge," said Hornsby, kindly, "I don't like to leave you, either, but you can't afford to turn down that kind of offer."

So Rog went to the Cubs for five players and $200,000. And, hitting .380 with thirty-nine homers and 149 RBIs, he won his second National League Most Valuable Player award as the Cubs won the pennant.

A YEAR LATER, however, at the Memorial Day milestone, Hornsby suffered a broken bone in his ankle, sliding, and missed out most of the run production ahead of Hack Wilson's hot bat. As mentioned earlier, the Cubs missed the pennant, too, and just before the season ended, Hornsby was named to succeed McCarthy as manager. Poor Joe, all he did then was to win eight pennants with the New York Yankees.

Slowed down a bit with the heavy-boozing, Wilson drowned his belief that Rog was "taking the bat out of my hands." Whether Hornsby's requiring Hack to take too many pitches in 1931 was critical, the sawed-off slugger fell off. So did the Cubs, finishing third. But Hornsby had the Cubs in first place in early August, 1932, with a 53-44 record, when the senior Veeck bounced him.

If ever a man needed to take Dale Carnegie's course on "How to Win Friends and Influence People," it was Mr. Blunt. He offended the front office and players, reportedly borrowing from some to pay off bets on slow horses and cold dice. When the Cubs perked up to play even better for Charley Grimm, and win a pennant, the players didn't even want to vote Rog any World Series share.

Rather than have enough money at thirty-seven to make it stick when he recommended changes of climate to the hottest for his employers, Hornsby was broke and needed a job. Rickey and Breadon let by-gones be. In 1933, they brought back the once-greatest righthand hitter who had been almost entirely a bench boss on the heel of the foot of the broken ankle.

If the Rajah only pinch-hit and played utility, fine. If, after Gelbert's injury, Frisch could play shortstop and his old rival second base, great.

Frisch, who had held out before to get a buck or to keep from losing one, recognized he had little bargaining position in view of his own poor season and the club's season. Also, the woeful economy. He wrote Gabby Street a reassuring letter, published by *The Sporting News:*

"I want you to know that you can count on my being in condition. I always was accustomed to skating and hunting in the winter, and my trip to Japan, while enjoyable, didn't do me any good. I took on weight and my muscles became flabby . . . I will promise you right now that I'll show the fans the greatest year they ever saw from old Frank. I'm good for some time yet, and you just put it down that I'll have one of the best years I ever had . . . "

Frisch wasn't THAT good any more, but he was a better-conditioned and, as a result, better ball player. Even so, he was told sorrowfully one day at Lake Placid, by the captain of the United States Olympic bobsled team, that the Flash couldn't flash down those swishing, delicate, weight-shifting turns with their two-man and four-man crews any longer.

"You're a professional, Frank, and you could jeopardize our amateur standing," said the bobsled skipper who had invited Frisch to participate in the first place.

"Gee, I'm sorry," the Flash lied through his teeth, relieved because, as he explained later, he'd been scared stiff, and yet too proud to admit it. "I'd looked forward so much to bobsledding again."

Over the years, Frisch's humor either developed or merely was reported more. For instance, although he was aware shortstop wasn't his bag and that he could make a fool of himself, he'd make the move for the good of the cause.

"But the experiment didn't last," he explained later, merrily, "because I didn't have a shortstop's sure hands or range to my right. And Rog didn't have the ability to go to his left too well from second base. So we both camped on the bag, which made us look like a couple of conventioneers. Clubby for Rog and me, but just plain murder for our pitchers."

Others tried at shortstop were little better than Frisch afield. Not so good at bat, the aging Flash still was superior to the older, tenderfooted Hornsby at second base. Ergo, Branch Rickey went to work.

On the road, writers traveling with the Cardinals were summoned to the general manager's suite at an early hour. Hair tousled B.R. sat in his bed in his pajamas, propped up after a full night on the telephone. The inner man craved reward for a job well done. With a breakfast tray of ham and eggs—the works, including a fresh cigar on which he would gnaw before taking a few winks with Morpheus and dream of Sid Weil—he brandished a fork with a home-fried potato and broke the news: He'd obtained Durocher to play shortstop.

The Lip, twenty-seven, fit like a glove, a Golden Glove next to Frisch. The Flash liked the alertness as well as the skill of the West Springfield, Massachusetts pool shark. Leo might owe everybody in Cincinnati, dressing like a million even when he was lucky to pay for a shoeshine on those expensive alligators, but he was something special in the long-sleeved uniform he wore with the number "2."

Playing shallowly, he had the knack of circling quickly to his right so that he could backhand a ball and come up throwing. You could win with a guy like Leo, thought Frisch, no matter if he wasn't much of a

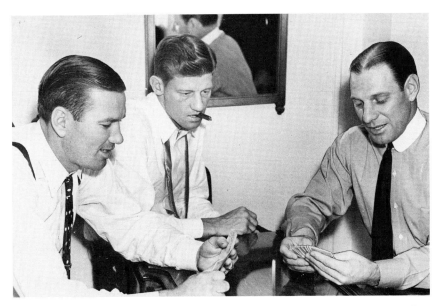

Slick and Sartorial: Leo Durocher, clever at playing cards and billiards as well as baseball, dressed the part, too, as obvious when he sat at the right of Dizzy Dean in a gin rummy game. The cigar-gnawing kibitzer is Lon Warneke.

hitter. Just get him to learn how to go to right field to give himself up by moving a runner along.

Street's ball club picked up. But then at the Polo Grounds it ran into humiliation and Carl Hubbell, a horrible combination. Before a 50,000-plus crowd on a Sunday, Hubbell lefthanded eighteen scoreless innings in a doubleheader opener. He didn't walk a man, facing Tex Carleton and then Pop Haines, before pulling off a 1-0 masterpiece. And with fast-firing Dizzy Dean going in the second-game gloaming against Tarzan Parmelee, who threw as hard as Ol' Diz, but not so accurately, the Giants' Johnny Vergez hit an early home run that held up for another 1-0 win for New York.

Proving that Hornsby could hit in the dark at midnight, the Rajah came off the bench to drill a base hit off Parmelee. But Durocher, although he'd battle you with fists, spikes or pool cue, had nervous feet against a guy you scarcely could see when it was daylight bright. Besides, Parmelee didn't know Gus Mancuso's target from the backstop screen.

Striking feebly, Leo hurried back to the St. Louis bench as the umpire called out, "Hey, you've got another strike coming."

Just like the Babe: Frank Frisch, gnawing a chunk of chewing tobacco, teed off on Alvin Crowder in the first major league All-Star game at Chicago's Comiskey Park, 1933, and hit a home run. Note the "NL" cap as the National League team that first year wore special gray, blue-trimmed uniforms.

Good Luck, Skip: Next page, ball players traditionally used to call managers "Skipper." The new skipper congratulated in July, 1933, was Frank Frisch. From the left, James (Tex) Carleton, Dizzy Dean, Pepper Martin, George Watkins, and the man who wanted the job as much as Frisch did, Jimmy Wilson.

"You take it," the amused Cardinals quoted the quick-quipping Durocher, who dutifully went back to swing through the ball and resume his retreat to the safety of the dugout.

By mid-July, the first All-Star baseball game had been promoted by *The Chicago Daily Tribune's* Arch Ward as a sideshow of Chicago's Century of Progress on the lakefront. Frisch, voted top second baseman by the nation's fans, started for his old mentor, Mr. McGraw, sentimentally brought out of retirement to manage against the American League patriarch, Connie Mack.

The game at Comiskey Park excited Frisch, who thought it had merit as an annual game to help indigent old-time ball players. The Flash, by the way, although he'd puff a cigar or a cigarette now and then, maintained he'd tried chewing tobacco and found it distasteful. But that isn't a billiard ball in the right cheek of the Flash as he was caught by a still photographer, swinging from his heels against Washington's twenty-four-game winner, righthanded Alvin Crowder, for an All-Star game home run. Frankie also singled.

In mock disgust he would reminisce after playing in just two All-Star games, hitting a home run from each side of the plate, and getting four

hits in seven trips: "Yeah, everybody remembers that Babe Ruth hit a homer in that first game, but nobody remembers that the poor old Flash did, too."

Frisch wasn't poor or unhappy, especially on July 24, 1933, when Sam Breadon announced that Street had been paid off as manager, and Frisch had been promoted to the job. At the time, Frank's old New York teammate, Bill Terry, who had taken over from McGraw the previous June and finished in a sixth-place tie with St. Louis, was headed toward a pennant. The Cardinals were fourth with a 46-45 record.

Breadon was aware of both the flouting of spring training curfew and conduct the previous year and of Street's apparent unwillingness to rely longer on his brain trust of veterans. He thought the Old Sarge had lost control. Street, in retort, charged he had not been backed by the management when, for instance, he'd sought in 1932 to fine Frisch $5,000 for "loafing."

Both Rickey and Breadon denied that such a fine had been proposed, acknowledging that, if it had, the sum would have been "unthinkable."

"I never heard that, but I hope it would have been unthinkable," said Frisch. "I took a salary cut alone that hurt. I apologized to Gabby for not having been in the best shape last year. To the club ownership, and to the fans, too, but I did not 'lay down.' Playing hurt, I simply couldn't go all-out on routine plays."

Frisch was aware that Brooklyn had shown interest in him as manager when Wilbert Robinson's long reign ended and that the Giants had inquired of Breadon about his availability even before McGraw quit in early 1932. He had hoped to manage eventually. Now, he said he was ready.

With Prohibition repealed, he said he'd see that beer was provided in the clubhouse. "I know players will drink, but I hope not to excess," he said. "I'd rather have them cool out over a beer in the clubhouse than charge out of a shower and into a bar where they might get into mischief."

He planned, Frisch said, to expand his pitching rotation, if possible, so that Dizzy Dean, a twenty-game winner who had struck out seventeen Cubs for a major league record at the time, would not be overworked.

"Mainly," said the Flash, "I want a hustling ball club, a team that will play 'Pepper Martin baseball,' that will take the extra base the way Pepper does. You know, a club that will run a slide and play as hard as Pepper does."

And drive the manager a little nutty, too.

14
Zoo's Zoo: The Gang Gathers

OVERCOAT COLLAR turned up in the face of a cold, biting wind in New York, Frank Frisch stood outside the steps of the church where the funeral Mass had been sung for John J. McGraw. February, 1934 would be memorable for "McGraw's Boy."

Yeah, the Fordham Flash was the Old Man's "boy" again. A couple of years or so earlier, Frank had been at the New York Athletic Club with wife Ada. The McGraws were hosts at a party across the dining room. Suddenly, lovely Blanche McGraw approached.

"Won't you come over, Frank," she said, "and say hello to John?"

The Dutchman, whom the Little Napoleon had called yellow, gutless, dumb, etc., back in 1926, was about to give it a smart aleck if-he-wants-to-see-me-let-him-come-over-here, when Ada put a gentle hand on his arm. "Do it, Frank," she said, "and you'll feel better, and Mr. McGraw, too."

Good-bye, Mr. Mac: *Frank Frisch, bundled against the cold of a New York February, attends the funeral of John McGraw in 1934.*

So Frisch did. And before the night was over, the Frisches were out at the McGraws' place at Pelham Park. Frankie and Johnny were talking about the good old days, remembering this triumph and that chuckle. The ice was broken.

When McGraw died of uremic poisoning and cancer of the prostate that reunion made the sorrow sweet rather than guilty. Now, the Flash's job was to beat that big bozo, Bill Terry, whose Giants had just won over Washington for the world championship.

In February, 1934, with a six-inch snowfall, St. Louis' heaviest in four years, planes were grounded, the stock market fluttered again, and even the big ones such as General Motors and U.S. Steel were down.

But to Frank Frisch, it was baseball time. Although the Flash's Cardinals had come home in 1933 exactly where he'd found them, meaning fifth place with a 268,404 attendance that was the club's poorest since 1919, the Redbirds had played those last sixty-two games by winning ten more than they had lost.

Frisch, who had once been paid $28,000 a season just to play second base, was now getting only $18,500 to both play and manage. A buck went a long way then. Besides, there was a sharp drop from Frankie's two-in-one salary to the $9,000 earned by two well-seasoned 1931 Series heroes, Pepper Martin and Bill Hallahan. Durocher, named by Frisch as captain for an extra $500, was getting $6,500 minus those multiple deductions to pay his debts. And that rookie battery of Paul Dean and Bill Delancey was paid just $3,000 each.

Indeed, the cast of characters Frisch confronted in the old wooden clubhouse, at what would become McKechnie Field in Bradenton, Florida, read like a Zoo's Zoo.

Delancey, and big Spud Davis were the catchers now. Jim Wilson, Frisch's old buddy, had had a falling out with Frank and had been traded to Philadelphia. There he'd been named player-manager.

Frankie and Jimmy had roomed together at times, dined on the road, and had been pals. When rumors began that Gabby Street would be replaced, Wilson said they'd each vowed to go all out for the other if the buddy took over. Obviously, Wilson thought he was as much in line for the job as Frisch.

"So what happened after we pledged the bond of friendship and cooperation?" the Ace complained at home in Philadelphia after the November deal. "Frisch worked my tail off, caught me in hot summer exhibition games and made it unpleasant for me. I thought he was a great guy, but he's a foul ball."

Shortly after Frisch took over in 1933, Rickey the psychologist had arranged for Rogers Hornsby, hitting .325 in infrequent appearances, to become player-manager of the rival St. Louis Browns. Frank and Rog got along well in the brief period the Flash managed the Rajah. And when Hornsby hit a home run in his first game for Frisch, Frank, coaching third base at the moment, had led the cheers.

"Attaboy, Rog," he said, giving Hornsby a vigorous handshake.

Still, it was a lot to ask one former superstar to play for the man he'd been traded for—and not just incidentally, on the club the first great had skippered.

The club had several colorful members, including Pepper Martin, who had converted to third base. All chest and wild-arm strong, Pepper had come to Florida in a pickup truck, looking like a refugee from John Steinbeck's *Grapes of Wrath.* The Oklahoman had dropped by St. Louis to soften up Branch Rickey, whose oratory he so admired and emulated.

He'd brought some fresh venison with him, knowing that Mr. Rickey liked game. They'd fallen to reminiscing. The general manager displayed his adroitness, especially when Pepper brought up how he'd moved full-time to third base the previous season and had rebounded to bat .316.

"Remember, Pepper," Rickey said, enjoying the evasion, "the time you came in here after your vaudeville tour, following the 1931 World Series? You had all of $10,000 cash on you, and I was worried, and said, 'Pepper, somebody might rob you.' Remember what you said?"

"Sure," recalled the muscular little man, "I said, 'No they won't.'"

If a holdup man had ever tried to take Johnny Leonard Roosevelt Martin's money, World War III would have started before World War II. He was a powerful, virile man. He wore no underwear, on or off the field. And he played third base, the hot corner, without even so much as a jockstrap, much less a protective cup.

The way Pepper ran the bases was almost as frightful for the foe as it was delightful for the fans. Frisch hadn't been whistling Dixie when he

The Ripper: *Jimmy (Rip) Collins, switch-hitting first baseman of the Gas House Gang, a part-time sports writer and a full-time prankster, was a perpetrator of many jokes.*

said he'd like to see an entire ball club diving around the way Martin did. Pep must have reminded the Flash of himself in his younger days, although Frisch was more cat-like.

The sights to behold of number "1," leadoff man Martin, were his inside-out swing that sliced the ball into right field, the slinging bat, his belly-flopping into a base, and his pounding his chest to rid himself of the dust as if he were a housewife beating a rug. The crowds loved it, just as they did the way the grimy guy ran to first base. Instead of striding onto and past the bag, slowing to a natural stop, he'd hit the base and skid to an abrupt halt, popping a spectator's knee ligaments vicariously.

Playing hard, Martin was subject to injuries. He'd be forced out now and then, but when he was in the game, he'd give it what Branch Rickey called "quantitative quality."

Lefty Collins, Jimmy the Ripper at first base, would dance those big, bulging blue eyes when he'd talk about Martin. Short for a first baseman, the Ripper wasn't much taller than the 5-foot-9 Wild Horse. He'd recall that there WAS a mean streak in the joyful, fun-loving third baseman.

"Pep hated 'em to bunt on him," said Collins, "and more than once, when they did, I've seen him charge the ball, grab it and throw at the runner rather than to first base. If you were hit by Pepper Martin, brother, you felt it."

At times, a comical sight was when Martin would stick that strong, hairy chest into the path of a hot smash, knock it down, just sort of "surround" the rebound, scoop it up and let it fly with all his might. Collins would be backing toward the right-field bull pen to retrieve the anticipated wild throw even before the ball sailed over his upraised mitt.

Collins, at thirty, was like Martin, a player who had been kept in the minors too long by the Cardinals' farm system. At the time, Breadon and Rickey had talent running out of their ears—talent, but not money—so they would sell what seemed to be surplus players.

For instance, they kept Bill DeLancey in '34, dealt Ken O'Dea to Chicago for cash, retained Paul Dean and sold Bill Lee to the Cubs. This was BIG Bill Lee, a right-handed pitcher not to be confused with the eccentric lefthanded Lee of more recent times.

BEFORE LONG, the Cardinals would wish they had both Lee and O'Dea. Illness struck down Delancey and injury overtook Paul Dean. But in '34, before Paul had thrown a ball for the Cardinals, brother Dizzy, three years older, was holding out for him. At a time when Diz was paid $7,500 himself, he was trying to get $5,000 for the kid. That is, until Paul, who spoke more softly as well as less often, made more sense if not dollars.

"Let me make that club first, Jay," he said, using the name favored by Dizzy's wife, Pat.

You see, although Rickey and Frisch and others more often than not addressed Dizzy as "Jerome," as in Jerome Herman, Dizzy was named properly Jay Hanna.

"After some Wall Street big shot," was the way he told the chief chronicler of the Gas House Gang, J. Roy Stockton, "or was he named for me?"

His other name came about when a neighbor lost his son, named Jerome Herman, through illness when Dizzy and his brothers were knee-high to a pig pen. Dean said, "Shucks, the nicest thing I could do for the poor man was to change my name to Jerome Herman so that he'd feel as if he might-a lost a son, but he'd-a gained one, too."

And that nickname, Dizzy, came from an Army sergeant when he was in Uncle Sam's peace-time khaki.

Good fella, that Dizzy. He was thoughtful to the press, also. Stockton did a triple take one trip in New York when he read three stories that gave three different birthdates, and three different birthplaces for the Great One.

"Well, I know how it is," Dizzy explained. "You gotta have different angles to your stories from the next guy, so I gave 'em each a scoop."

To one writer, Dizzy Dean said he'd been born on January 16, 1911 at Lucas, Arkansas. To another it was August 22, Holdenville, Oklahoma. And to the third, it was February 22, in Bond, Mississippi.

A Peach of a Pair: *A good-hitting team of catchers, rookie Bill DeLancey (right), and line-drive hitting veteran batter Virgil (Spud) Davis.*

"I figure," explained Ol' Diz, "that I'd give my wife's folks a break by naming Bond and also George Washington, too, because he was the Father of our country. But I wasn't sure about the other two until Pa said it was Lucasville on January 16. Since he was there, too, I guess he might know."

By the time the 1934 clan gathered in the clubhouse, John McGraw, Jr., as Cardinals called Frisch behind his back, had it fixed in his mind that the Redbirds could rebound from two second-division seasons. His good friend and former New York teammate, Mike Gonzalez, a tall, jug-eared, good-field, no-hit catcher with big feet, and a memory to match, had told him to watch what "Mike, she tole you" about the two kids he'd seen at Columbus the previous year, Paul Dean and Bill Delancey.

Said Gonzalez, who would be the Flash's third-base coach, "You stay with Pablo, Frohnk, and she can do. Dee, she catch like Mike and hit like you, only harder."

Frisch thought the potential of another pitcher and a lefthanded-hitting catcher with pop in his bat would do wonders for the Cardinals. The Flash had this thing about catchers.

"If I were starting a ball club," he explained years later, "and had my pick of players by positions, I'd get the best possible shortstop, then a helluva center fielder, and a good second baseman. My next two would be catchers, one to hit righthanded, the other lefthanded. A fresh catcher and one with punch against the kind of pitcher you're facing on a given day is great for a ball club's morale, and its muscle."

However, at the outset in 1934, Frisch did not know how DeLancey or Paul Dean would fare in big league ball, a seven-league stride farther than the best of the minor leagues when every hamlet had a professional ball club. From the outset, he liked outfield candidate Jack Rothrock, a retread from the American League's droopy Boston Red Sox of the period.

Rothrock knew how to run the bases, how to make the plays, how to throw; all dear to the heart of Frisch, a perfectionist himself. Besides, like the Flash and Ripper Collins, Jack (or Johnny, as some called him) was a switcher.

Only Brooklyn's Lee Magee had been a turn-around hitter when the Flash came up in 1919, Frankie recalled. The skipper liked it that three of his first five batters hit from either side of the plate.

Frisch, bedeviled by the rascals in Redbird uniforms, liked to tease. But he wasn't adverse to putting himself on, either. For instance, his retort when a few of the more courageous imitated the Old Flash trying to hit long-wristed Carl Hubbell's screwball.

Hub's screwball fell off the table against righthanded hitters, low and away. To manager Frisch's pleasure and player Frisch's disgust, Ernie Orsatti, his Hollywood center fielder, a lefthanded batter, hit Hub well.

One time, in desperation against Hubbell, Frisch turned around and batted lefthanded, which required looking most unusually at a curve ball breaking away from him. But, at least, lefthanded, that screwjie didn't up and die—kerplunk!—on the outside corner.

"Reminds me of the time I got four hits off Hub in five tries, and damned near fainted," Frankie recalled, "or the time I had an injured left wrist and batted lefthanded against Watty Clark, pretty good Brooklyn lefthander. Got three hits.

An Old Pro: *Johnny (Jack) Rothrock, a retread from the Boston Red Sox by way of the minors, played all Redbird games in 1934. A good, switch-hitting second-place batter and steady, Rothrock was Frisch's choice as an unsung standout.*

"But," the Flash smiled, "I'm still the only guy in baseball history to take three pitches from each side of the plate one time at bat. Against [the same] Clark, the count went to '3-and-0' when Brooklyn made a pitching change and brought in Hollis Thurston, a righthander.

"Oh, how the Old Flash loved to hit Sloppy Thurston! I turned around to bat lefthanded, licking my chops, and—know what?—that such-and-such threw me the best-looking lollipop curves I ever saw. And I took each one of them for a strike. Three balls righthanded, three strikes—and out—lefthanded."

But Frisch wasn't in a reminiscing or playful mood as he faced the Cardinals at the start of spring training in 1934. He looked around at familiar faces—Dizzy, Pepper, Leo, Joe, Pop, the two Bills (Hallahan and Walker) and the new ones such as DeLancey, Paul Dean, and that good-looking Phi Beta Kappa groomed to replace the Flash, Burgess Whitehead.

"Listen you guys,"———it could have been McGraw talking, not his "boy"———"We're going to win this pennant. If those bozos Terry has got in New York could go that far, so can we. I don't mind a bit of horseplay, but I want an honest day's work and beardown baseball from you.

"We're going to work two-a-day, so put away those golf clubs, and you're going to walk to and from the hotel [the Dixie Grande]. I believe running is the best exercise you can get, and walking the second best.

"Now, if you think I'm tough, just ask Mike [Gonzalez] about McGraw. The Old Man made us walk two miles each way. If we wanted to get dressed and leave the park for lunch, we'd get our butts fined if he found out, which he ALWAYS did, that we'd grabbed a streetcar or hitched a ride.

"I'm going to be easier than McGraw was. We used to have an intra-squad game the first day. One year, because it was tied after six innings, we had to go fifteen to a decision. If you're hurt, let me know before you leave the field, and Doc [Weaver] will take it from there. He's the best—even if I think he's a bush leaguer on the mandolin."

A titter, and spike shuffling, and smiles, but they faded as the Flash's voice became shrill as it did when he was angry.

"If any of you humpty-dumpties don't think we can win, turn in your jock straps now, and Clarence Lloyd will get you your train ticket back to the coal mines or farm, or wherever the else you can starve these days. Mr. Breadon feeds you buzzards pretty damned good. So, take your choice: Play to win, or get your rear ends out of here and into the bread lines. Now, let's go!"

Dizzy Dean, a ripe old twenty-three, spoke up enthusiastically.

"You said a mouthful, Frank," piped up the big-name, big-game pitcher.

15
Fists and Fun

THE HIJINKS and low comedy of the Gas House Gang began in spring training, 1934. It intensified after Dizzy Dean breezed past an old nemesis, Pittsburgh, in the season opener. And that bronzed, hard-hitting young left fielder, Joe Medwick, teed off an even more troublesome pain in the standings, Heine Meine.

Meine ran a saloon in suburban St. Louis South County. His soft-throwing righthanded junk repeatedly troubled the Redbirds, but not the Hungarian Rhapsody or Muscular Magyar, as the more poetic in the press box labeled Medwick. Joe hit a two-run blast opening day and continued on to a good season of eighteen homers, 106 RBIs, and .319.

But the biggest seasons were still ahead of the twenty-two-year-old kid from Cartaret, New Jersey. He was such a good football player that even Knute Rockne at Notre Dame had been interested in him before Muscles began to play pro ball under the name of "Mickey King" to protect his amateur standing.

121

Jersey Joe: Medwick married lovely Isabel Heutel in August 1936, and manager Frisch stayed away so his team could have fun. Iz's brother, Harry Heutel, at left, is followed by Cardinals Charley Gelbert, Ed Heusser, Leo Durocher (best man) Medwick, Jesse Haines, the bride, Terry Moore, coaches Clyde (Buzzy) Wares, and Mike Gonzalez (shaking Joe's hand), Leroy (Bud) Parmalee, and Spud Davis.

Joey, as Frank Frisch called him, wasn't one of the funnier men in the St. Louis heavy baseball flannels. He did his hitting with that big black bat, hitching his front leg and belting the ball from foul-line to foul-line. He was such a good bad-ball hitter that his weakness was probably one right down the middle, or maybe, a pitch thrown UNDER the plate.

Medwick married lovely, olive-skinned Isabel Heutel late in the 1936 season, with Leo Durocher as his best man. Both before and after that day, the Beau Brummell shortstop was Medwick's mentor, smoothing out the crudeness of the immigrant's son, and getting him into the conservative well-cut clothes favored by the dapper twenty-eight-year-old Lip himself.

But no one could take the sass out of the truculent Medwick, whose salary disputes became annual as he turned on the power. Hitting .353, and .351 he finally became the National League's most recent Triple Crown batting champion when in 1937 he walloped 237 hits, including fifty-six doubles, ten triples and thirty-one home runs. The homers, like his 154 RBIs and .374 average, led the league.

Later, Medwick would muse, "That Rickey would do anything to get you to sign. Ever talk contract with a man who is shaving himself with a straight razor—without shaving cream? My God, I thought I'd seen more blood than Count Dracula."

After that tremendous season, Ducky Wucky showed that he did indeed have a sense of humor even if it was more sarcastic than "Frankie's," as the kid referred to the thirty-seven-year-old Frisch.

"Now, Mr. Rickey," Medwick said, tauntingly, at the ball club offices for a salary session, "I'd like to know what I did wrong?"

"Harumph," grumbled the general manager, "I suggest you see Sam Breadon . . . "

The next year, one of chaos for the Cardinals, Medwick had the misfortune to drop to .322. The figure was still robust enough to make most hitters drool, especially with his twenty-one homers and 122 RBIs. Predictably, the penny-pinching Cardinals offered a salary cut. Bypassing Rickey, Medwick waged wages' war with Breadon. Suddenly, just $2,000 was at issue.

Breadon said, "It's a matter of principle with me, Joe, not principal. I'd just as soon throw the $2,000 out of this office window."

Medwick laughed, which you didn't do in Sam Breadon's face very often, and said disrespectfully, "Mr. Breadon, if you ever threw $2,000 out the window, your arm would still be holding onto it."

Basically, though, Muscles fought more than he talked. In the batting cage one day, he decked tall righthanded pitcher Tex Carleton for taking too much time that Joe felt belonged to the regulars. At New York's Polo Grounds, right in the dugout, he felled Ed Heusser, a pretty tough hombre, because the Wild Elk of the Wasatch criticized Medwick's outfielding.

At Pittsburgh, where Dizzy Dean thought Joe had short-legged it on a fly that fell in for a three-run double, the Great One huffed angrily into the bench after the inning. Dizzy and Joe exchanged unpleasantries from one end of the dugout to the other. Suddenly, the brothers Dean, Dizzy and Paul, were advancing with loud clicking spiked shoes toward Medwick.

Let Durocher tell it as he did loudly with a rasping baritone in the present-tense formerly favored by ball players:

"Joey picks up that big black bat of his and says, 'All right, step right up, boys, and I'll separate you.'"

Jay Dean's beef with Medwick was that "he don't fight fair."

"All a guy wants to do is sound off with a little chin music and before you can open your mouth, that Joe whomps you. Ain't fair."

But Joe whomped the ball even more. Next time up, he hit a grand-slam homer over Forbes Field's ivy-covered brick wall, trotted back to the bench with head down and stopped at the water cooler for a sip of water.

He filled his mouth and walked over to where Dizzy Dean sat. Medwick spat the water on the pitcher's kangaroo-hide shoes and said, "All right, you big meathead, there's your three runs back and one extra. Let's see you hold the damned lead."

Frisch, who felt like he was part fight-manager, part promoter, part player, and, oh, yes, part baseball pilot, finally resolved it when Medwick swung in the clubhouse at the first-base pixie, Rip Collins. The Flash kept teammates from breaking it up, and let Medwick and Collins punch themselves out until they were arm weary.

Then, throwing an arm around each of his huffing gladiators, Frisch grinned. "All right," he said, "kiss and make up. I mean, shake hands. Dammit, fellows, you're on the same side. Let's fight the opposition more, and each other less."

Wise counsel if not a cure-all. But then, one time in 1934, after a particularly stinging episode with the Dean brothers over a suspension in which, as always, Dizzy was the ring-leader, brother Paul surprised him by saying:

"Jay, why don't you punch that old Dutchman right between the eyes?"

Johnny on the Spot: Johnny (Pepper) Martin leaped in to restrain powerful Pittsburgh catcher Al Todd, but Paul Dean appeared to be ready to fight for his honor at St. Louis' old Sportsman's Park in 1934.

IF FRISCH made a contribution to his Cardinals in 1934, the year Rickey, as mentioned, would have dealt him to Boston in spring training for catcher Al Spohrer, it was in playing 140 games at a pace better than B.R. believed, hitting .304, a point higher than in '33. But mostly, his contribution was in the patience Frisch showed with his jock-strapped menagerie, particularly in the care, feeding and development of Paul Dean.

Now, Mama and Herr Frisch, both of whom lived into their eighties to see son Franz become a star player and winning manager, hadn't raised a fool for Fordham to educate. The Flash was aware that there was boxoffice potential in having brother pitchers, particularly when one already was as colorful as Dizzy.

Dean had the delightful habit of making good-natured boasts come true. But he'd seemed to over-reach himself in spring training when he prophesied, "If they give the kid the ball often enough, me 'n Paul will win forty-five games."

Paul Dee Dean, like Jay Hanna, had been born in Arkansas, a couple of years after Dizzy. Paul had played ball from way back, usually as a shortstop behind his older brother. In 1931, the year Dizzy got married, Paul signed for a ham sandwich, or its modest equivalent, to get the heck off Pa Dean's itinerant cotton-choppin' merry-go-round. In 1932 he'd had only a 7-16 record with Columbus in the American Association. Then he blossomed forth with a 22-and-7 record.

An even six feet, 180 pounds, long-jawed, and with heavy lower legs that would make him subject to shin splints, Paul wasn't quite so tall or gangly as an early-day Dizzy, although both eventually would eat themselves into astonishing corpulence.

When Robert E. Hood was ferreting facts for his 1976 book, *The Gas House Gang,* published by William Morrow and Company of New York, he went to Birmingham, Alabama, for a talk with Virgil (Spud) Davis, who caught for the 1934 Cardinals, later a coach for Frisch at Pittsburgh. Spud noted that Dizzy had the better curve ball and change-up.

"He threw a rising fast ball and could do everything. He was a natural, a pretty good hitter and he ran the bases. Paul threw a heavy fast ball. It was like catching a ton of bricks."

But it looked early in the 1934 season as if Paul Dean were destined to flop like a ton of bricks. Frisch started him once. Batted out. Twice. Batted out. Three times. Batted out. If he hadn't been named Dean, would he have been given a fourth chance? Maybe not, but, then, stylish Bill Walker, the East St. Louis southpaw who looked like the Duke of Windsor, suffered a broken arm. And that year, Bill Hallahan was largely Wild Bill, not Sweet William.

So with the Cardinals floundering and the world champion New York Giants in town, Frisch started Paul again on a Ladies' Day in mid-May against crafty Carl Hubbell, the twenty-three-game meal ticket of the mound for Bill Terry.

Paul started shakily, but got out of the first inning. In the home half, Pepper Martin led off with a double to left, belly-flopping into second. With one out, Frisch hit one to right-center, went into the remnant of his old Man O' War gallop and slid headfirst into third with a triple. Paul Dean, just twenty, hung in there and went all the way. He won in ten innings, 3-2.

So as one prize rookie began to pay off, so did another. On Memorial Day, Bill DeLancey caught at Cincinnati and had four hits, including a home run and a triple. The tall, knock-kneed lefthanded hitter who wore his cap at a rakish angle, began to move into the lineup as the number one catcher.

Before long, Dizzy Dean would not pitch to Davis. He wanted as catcher the twenty-two-year-old Carolinian who could hit with power and throw the same way. Talk tough, too. When Dizzy was horsing around one day, which he would do at times with a sizable lead, DeLancey zinged the ball back to the mound harder than Dizzy had thrown it. It was followed with a "hint" to the mouth-gaping big man.

"Listen, you long-legged so-and-so, you may be a big shot," said the kid, "but if you ever throw any of that crap again when I'm catching, I'll knock you right on your seat."

Dean loved the comeuppance. He'd clown, but not when the man in the mask and mitt was number "9." DeLancey, whose fire caught the fancy of Frisch, was a hard loser, too.

The Old Flash liked to recall how he'd tried to advise the lefthanded-hitting slugger to lay off change-ups down around his knees unless he had two strikes. "You're off stride when the pitcher lets up, Dee, and you pop up," said Frisch.

One day at Cincinnati, timing a change of pace, DeLancey hit it over the fence for a homerun, trotted around the bases, accepted teammates' congratulations, and, sitting some distance from Frisch, said, loud enough for the manager of fifteen seasons to hear:

"I wonder how the Dutch bleep liked that one?"

Dee hit .316 and 13 homers in 93 games.

When the Gang wasn't running roughshod into the foe or taking punches at each other, they were dangerously playful. In one silly wrestling match in the clubhouse, bosom buddies Dizzy Dean and Pepper Martin took time off from coaching the batboy with boxing ambitions, Kayo Brown, to grapple catch-as-catch-ouch!

"My God," gasped Frisch, pulling at his thinning hair as Dizzy flexed his valuable right arm, which had been wrenched.

Another time, Martin came into the clubhouse more disheveled than usual, a sharp contrast to such snappy dressers as Durocher, Medwick and Ernie Orsatti. Frisch thought Pepper had been in a fight.

"No, Frank, but I fell down in a foot race and still beat the other guy."

"A foot race? Why?"

"To win a bet."

A Lira for His Thoughts:
Ernie Orsatti, Hollywood-
oriented outfielder, strikes
a pensive pose in front of
the Cardinals' dugout.

"What kind of bet?"

"Two gallons of ice cream," the big-beaked Oklahoman said, triumphantly.

Pepper didn't need much urging, but he had the kind of behind-the-scenes' direction from that sneaky rascal, Collins or from Orsatti, a Hollywood double for silent comic Buster Keaton and brother of movie agent Frank Orsatti.

Ernie once got all of the guys a few bucks. One day in 1934, spectators at Sportsman's Park—and they weren't too numerous except when the Giants or Cubs were in town—were puzzled before a game to see action.

Orsatti, swinging at a pitch, hit to left-center. As an "opposing" player bobbled the ball, Ernie raced around the bases. Then, near home plate, he "collapsed" as Cardinal teammates rushed out of the dugout.

Unknown to the crowd, it was a scene for a movie called "Death on the Diamond," starring television's latter-day Dr. Welby, a young Robert Young, and lovely Madge Evans. Orsatti presumably had been "killed," shot by a mysterious villain in the story—the groundskeeper.

Orsatti drove a cream-colored Auburn roadster with red-leather up-holstery, parked right outside the Spring Avenue press gate. A friendly policeman kept a sharp eye on the car for a friendly guy. Ernie was a good lefthanded hitter, a handyman who tumbled often to make easy chances look hard, but he really didn't belong in center field. Still, dark hair slicked back as if Valentino were still alive, he cut a handsome figure and looked big leaguer.

Frisch knew the likable Italian had friends everywhere. And he'd tried to make certain Orsatti didn't break the curfew or bend it too much. But Ern outsmarted him. At a hotel, Orsatti would slip the phone operator a couple of bucks, and coax her to direct all his calls to the hotel's supper club.

After midnight, Frisch would give him a jingle and, yawning from a table with friends, Orsatti would feign sleep arousal and protest, "Gee, Frank, what's wrong?"

Just checking, Orsatti would be told, and, by the way, Frisch would wonder, what was that music in the background?

"Oh," Ernie would say sweetly, "I was reading in bed and forgot to turn off the radio."

Yeah, the contretemps of the cutthroat cutups was well-orchestrated. It went like this:

Rip Collins would suggest to Pepper Martin that wouldn't it be fun to put sneezing powder in the hotel lobby?

Wouldn't it be even funnier to feign a fight in the lobby with Dizzy? They'd secret popcorn in each mouth so that when the two men swung, the white stuff they'd flip out would look like teeth?

And say, Johnny, wasn't that Frisch standing outside the hotel, wearing no hat on a balmy summer night in Boston? Wouldn't that bald spot make a perfect bombs-away target for a paper bag dropped from above, full of water?

More than once the water would splash next to Frisch in a day before polyester built-in pants' creases. Try as the Old Flash might to catch the culprit, he'd rush into the lobby, but Pepper would always beat him and, as a result, would look as innocent, frowning as he sat "studying" the evening newspaper.

VICTORY was the big thing. Besides, Frisch knew that the most accurate bombardier was Rip Collins. He knew, too, that it was the first baseman who had engineered one of the most amusing gags.

At Philadelphia's staid Bellevue-Stratford, a luncheon was interrupted one day by, of all things, painters who walked in, talked loudly, as a "superintendent" issued orders to move this table and that one, to cover the lectern, and . . .

Just before an irate master of ceremonies could call the hotel management, someone recognized Dizzy Dean, Pepper Martin and Rip Collins,

The Wild Horse at Bay: *Pepper Martin sucks in the strong stomach that used to knock down line drives at third base.*

all dressed in painters' gear they'd spotted down the hall. Amid a good belly laugh, the three Redbirds just had to oblige with a few words.

A few words was a lot to ask of Dizzy. That is, it was a lot to ask him to say so little. If Rip Collins, Ol' Diz and the others could have gone beyond KMOX radio with Pepper's favorite song, "Birmingham Jail" or Dizzy's trademarked "Wabash Cannonball," they'd certainly have made a lot more money. And if television, guest shots and talk shows had been available before Pepper Martin's Mudcat Band was created, just think of the loot they'd have carried off to supplement skimpy salaries!

When the 1934 Gang got together in 1959, Branch Rickey chuckled at their mischief. He extolled their "sense of adventure" and suggested "they loved the game so much that they would have played for nothing." Martin got up immediately after B.R. and said, "John Brown, Mr. Rickey, we darn near did!"

Open-faced, hard-playing, but free and easy, rough and yet gentle, Pepper Martin had a way of getting in the last word—except when it came to his devotion for his dear wife, Ruby. A few years later, straying off the alcoholic reservation briefly, Pep tore up a Georgia town in a one-man, strong-armed spree on a spring-training barnstorming trip north.

Leo Ward, then the Cardinals' young traveling secretary, came upon the scene, horrified, to find a trigger-happy hamlet sheriff with revolver drawn. The law man was prepared to shoot the powerful athlete who defied orders to get into a jail cell and sleep it off. Ward, too, found Martin outraged, militant and menacing. Until, that is, Leo said the magic words.

"Johnny," he said, "what if Ruby hears about this?"

Pepper's weathered features blanched, and he began to sob.

"No, please, no, please don't tell Ruby." Suddenly sobered and peaceful, Pepper permitted Ward to lead him out of the jail as the southern sheriff told the Sec to make damned certain the ball player stayed on the club's private Pullmans until a train pulled them out of town past midnight.

Pepper was a boy at heart, a rough-hewn boy. When he later managed Sacramento of the Pacific Coast League for the Cardinals and when weather interfered with spring training, he improvised deliciously. He took his guys indoors to play basketball. Well enough, but then he picked up the ball, stuck it under his arm like a football and stiff-armed Buddy Blattner and the rest of the kids who tried to impede his progress to the opposite basket.

Until Frisch and Branch Rickey got him to cease, he not only managed a fair fighter named Junior Munsell, but Pepper also owned and drove a midget auto racer. Top management shuddered in concert to see Pepper and good ol' Dizzy grunting and groaning as they pushed Martin's car around a midget auto-race track at old Walsh Stadium in St. Louis.

One evening in New York after a tough loss that John McGraw, Jr. thought was especially stupid, Frisch pulled Muggsy's trick of keeping his men seated in sweaty uniforms that cooled clammily in a stuffy, steaming clubhouse as he harangued toward darkness.

Finally, Martin spoke up. "Frank," he said politely, "can I ask a question?"

"What?" was Frisch's growled answer.

Gravely, Johnny Leonard Roosevelt Martin said, "I wonder if I ought to paint my midget auto red with white wheels, or white with red wheels?"

The players snickered. Frisch's teeth showed in that rabbit grin the Old Flash couldn't conceal. All belly-laughed.

"Get to hell out of here, you guys," said Frisch with a smirk. "Especially you, Martin!"

The Wheel of Chance: *One of the reasons Frank Frisch's hair fell out was when Pepper Martin roared around the tracks in his midget auto racer.*

16
Me 'n Paul—
and Patooie!

IF FRANK FRISCH hadn't held his ground stubbornly handling Dizzy
Dean, as determinedly as handling a hot smash, the team aspects of an
essentially individual sport might not have paid off for St. Louis in 1934.
A ball club that became a legend might have faded into the mist of time
as just a collection of kooks and characters, interesting non-winners.

That year, twin disasters of the Depression and drought whipsawed
the land. In St. Louis alone, 217 persons died of heat prostration in July.
Air-conditioning then was only in downtown movie houses.

Dizzy Dean, who could do anything better than anybody else, insisted
he'd lost seventeen pounds in one game. Bob Hood, the Gas House
Gang researcher, reported that Carl Hubbell, whose pants hung down
low because Hub lamented he had no behind, called coming to St. Louis
riding "into the Valley of Death."

Another Hall of Famer, Al Lopez, the Brooklyn, Boston and Pittsburgh catcher who became a great manager at Cleveland and with the Chicago White Sox, would remember it to me this way:

"You'd come out of Boston with a cool breeze off the Charles River into the cauldron of the Mississippi Valley, and the Cardinals would psyche you out. Sure, they had to be hot, playing there three and four weeks at a time when clubs made fewer trips and longer ones. Somehow, they'd get used to it or pretend they did, anyway.

"That crazy Pepper Martin and Dizzy Dean—hell, Paul never was Daffy—they'd build a bonfire in front of the dugout on a Ladies' Day and put Indian blankets around their shoulders and squat, rubbing their hands together over the fire as if they were cold. Yet Hal Schumacher of the Giants damned near died of heat exhaustion pitching there. Would have, too, if Doc Hyland [Dr. Robert F. Hyland] hadn't been there.

"They'd go into that silly, sleight-of-hand pepper game. Something like the Harlem Globe Trotters of baseball. Pepper (Martin), and Rip Collins and Jack Rothrock or Ernie Orsatti would line, up, side by side, to field bunts. Then they'd flip the ball around their shoulders, under their legs, kick it, juggle it. Sitting on the other bench, you didn't know whether to laugh or cry—laugh because it was funny or cry because you knew it was 100 in the shade and those jokers were acting as if it was opening day."

Lopez, the man for whom Tampa's ball park is named, remembered that the Cardinals' infield would often put on a phantom drill. They'd snap up grounders and whip throws around—or pretend they did.

"They were great," said Lopez, smiling, "especially because they weren't using a ball."

When they did employ a "pelota," as coach Mike Gonzalez had them all using Spanish for "ball," two powerful-throwing infielders, Frisch and Martin, would wind up infield practice with a burn-out session. They'd throw the ball as hard as they could at each other. Frisch threw the harder or, at least, diplomatically, Pepper let the boss think he did. Finally, to the crowd's delight, Martin would retreat from third base, ultimately to the grandstand wall, where he'd climb over into the box seats, climaxing the act.

Then they'd go out and win or lose. They didn't win enough to more than just threaten Terry's staid Giants.

Dean was a riot. Once, he walked the likely last out to get to Terry, one of baseball's greatest hitters, because Diz had been to a hospital that morning and, offering to please the kids, had promised to strike out the Giants' manager.

"I hate to do this, Bill," said Ol' Diz, walking toward the plate to tell Terry, "but I promised the kids I'd strike you out."

He did, too. At times Dizzy would throw at the hitters because he was a competitive cuss. If they dug in firmly at the plate, the fast-working righthander with the flowing three-quarter delivery would smile and say,

"Take your time, podnuh, and dig that hole deep 'cause Ol' Diz is going to bury you in it."

Another time he invaded the oppositions' clubhouse and said to Brooklyn's Casey Stengel, going over the Cardinals' hitters in a closed meeting, "Don't mind me, Case, 'cause Ol' Diz knows how to pitch to 'em, too, and you're right. 'Sides, fair's fair, and when you're through, I'll tell you how I'm going to pitch to your fellas."

One game he told the Boston Braves he would use only a fast ball—"honest"—and did and won.

But he could be petulant and selfish, too. As far back as 1932, his rookie season, he'd wound up "by accident" on a Pullman at Pittsburgh, where the Cardinals would play next, rather than at Elmira, New York, where they had an exhibition scheduled. He begged out of a $100 fine levied by Gabby Street by promising to shut out the Pirates. And did.

In '34, however, just after he and Paul had lost a Sunday doubleheader at St. Louis to the Cubs, he told excellent pinch-hitter Pat Crawford that he'd be darned if he'd go to Detroit, where the Cardinals were scheduled to play the American League-leading Tigers for a children's benefit. He was seen picnicking while the others struggled to play the exhibition. The aging Frisch, who had gone eighteen hard-playing, futile innings the day before, acidly recalled that neither of the Deans had gone nine. He fined them $100 each. And Dizzy, to show his displeasure, tore up a uniform in the clubhouse. To oblige a photographer who'd missed it, he tore up another one.

When club treasurer Bill DeWitt billed him $36 for the uniforms, Dean refused to suit up.

"I understand the Dutchman is good with a needle and thread," he said.

When Frisch ordered the brothers into uniform and they refused, the manager fined both and suspended them for ten days. Breadon and Rickey upheld the manager, who appealed in a clubhouse meeting to what was left of a roster that had numbered only twenty-one players, two under the Depression limit. With Martin hurt, Frisch had moved over to third, using Burgess Whitehead at second base. The Cardinals had only eighteen able-bodied players, and two of them were really long in the tooth. Pitchers Dazzy Vance was forty-three and Jesse Haines forty.

"Dammit," said Frisch in a clubhouse meeting, spitting into his little glove and rubbing in the moisture mechanically as he talked, "NOBODY, but nobody, is bigger than this game."

The Gang came through. Bill Walker was back. He helped. Bill Hallahan came out of his slump. The old geezers, Vance and Haines did, too, and Tex Carleton. The team won eight out of nine. Then the high commissioner, Judge Landis, came to St. Louis for a hearing, to make certain that the ball club had been fair to the players. It had, he decided on August 20. Dizzy was out seven days' pay, plus $36 for those two torn-up uniforms.

The late-morning meeting went into figurative extra innings, lasting so long that a makeup doubleheader against Philadelphia began with seldom-seen third-string catcher Francis (Father) Healy at third base, listed in Frisch's third spot in the batting order. Durocher had to edge over from shortstop after each hitter in the first inning to tell Healy where to stand.

MAKESHIFT major league baseball at best, but it worked. Just as Healy prepared to step into the batter's box in the home half, Frisch emerged from the third base dugout buttoning his uniform shirt—no zippers then, no slipover, form-fitting jersey-type uniform tops—and Frank carried a bat.

Ample and affable field announcer Jim Kelley intoned over his giant, hand-held megaphone, "For the Cardinals, number "3," Frisch batting for . . ."

Uncle Frank, as they were beginning to call him, or Onkel Franz, as friend John Kieran dutched it up in *The New York Times*, got a base hit and then fielded sensationally in a doubleheader sweep. Durocher, facetiously called "Captain Slug" by Roy Stockton because he hit better in a jam, won the first game in eleven innings with a double.

So a penitent Dizzy Dean came back. He immediately shut out the Giants in late August, but the Cardinals trailed by seven and one-half games after they lost both ends of a Labor Day doubleheader at Pittsburgh. The Giants seemed to be in.

"Listen, you blockheads," Frisch raved as the final eastern swing began the next day at Brooklyn, "don't quit on me now, but, more important, don't quit on yourselves. Hell, I remember 1921, when the Pirates thought they had us buried in New York and—hey, Pop [Haines] and Bill [Hallahan] can tell you how we were supposed to be dead in 1930 and won."

Trite but true. The team that won't be beaten can't be beat, particularly if the team, the guy, or the horse in front stops running.

By mid-September, the Cardinals had cut the New York lead to four and one-half games after Paul Dean went twelve innings to win at the Polo Grounds, beating Fred Fitzsimmons. But when Hal Schumacher topped the Cards the next day, the Giants led by five and one-half with only fourteen to play.

Still, after a postponement, an overflow crowd filled the Giants' stadium at the Harlem River. Bud Parmelee led into the seventh, beating Dizzy Dean, 3-0. But then the fast-firing Parmelee weakened. Suddenly, with the bases loaded, two out, the Cards were down by a run. Manager Frankie Frisch, who had won many games over the years, both for the Giants and against them, found himself facing Schumacher in relief.

"I was so tired," Frisch would recall. "The bat felt so heavy, and don't let anybody tell you that, with age and fatigue, your eyes don't go just as your legs do."

But the old money player struck. The Flash singled to right, driving in the tying and go-ahead runs. The Cardinals added one more to win, 5-3. In the second game, Pepper Martin sliced an eleventh-inning homer to give Paul Dean his second extra-inning victory in the series, 3-1, over the great Hubbell.

So now it was three and one-half games. And after a successful series at Boston, St. Louis received sporting permission from Bill Terry, the New York manager, to stop over at Brooklyn for a makeup double-header. That's the day Dizzy Dean was reportedly told by Frisch, when going over the hitters, to pitch Tony Cuccinello one way when Dizzy wanted to do it another.

"Frank, I don't see how a little old infielder like you could tell a great pitcher like me how to pitch to any hitter," he said.

Frisch denied that yarn, but Dean didn't. With amusement, Frisch did tell how he'd called every pitch from second base.

"That big jughead didn't know that I had a system of signs worked out with DeLancey behind the plate so that Bill would look past Diz to me, to get each pitch. I'd give it quickly, hoping the opposition didn't catch on or Dizzy, either. The other side could have used it, I guess. For one, I never liked to be tipped what was coming, not after I was skulled with a fastball when I was a young fellow expecting a curve."

Pitching Cuccinello his way with Frisch's signs, Dizzy three-hitted the Dodgers in a first-game runaway, 13-0. Then brother Paul became the first rookie to work a no-hitter, 3-0.

Brooklyn's third-base coach, manager Casey Stengel, moaned, "Eighteen innings and I ain't seen a friendly face over here all day."

Dizzy was apologetic. "Gee whiz," he said, "if I'd-a known Paul was gonna do it [throw a no-hitter], I'd-a done it, too."

Over the years, Frank Frisch became short in memory for details because he'd played so many games. But he remembered one stretch-drive game vividly for cause and effect, if not for details.

"It was at Cincinnati," Frisch recalled, "just after we'd come out of the east. We had a chance to win from the Reds, but with runners on second and third, someone hit back to our pitcher along the third-base line. He cut over to field the ball, and I hurried over to back up first base. But the pitcher's throw was wild. It got by Collins and it got by me, too, rolling down toward the right-field bull pen. I never ran so fast in my life—or thought I did, anyway—and every step of the way, I'm saying, 'There goes the damned pennant . . . there goes the damned pennant.' "

Frisch finally caught up with the ball, fired hard, and accurately to the plate, but it was too late. The game was gone.

The game was gone, but not the race. Over at Chicago, with a chance to cut New York's lead to two games, Lefty Walker had the Cubs beat in the ninth, 3-2, backed by brilliant fielding. Chicago had the bases loaded, two out, right-handed Gabby Hartnett at the plate. There was a full count on the slugger.

"Gad, I couldn't use Dizzy and Paul EVERY day," said Frisch, "even though they pitched five of our last nine games. So from second base, I signaled for a curveball. I could see DeLancey stiffen, and I was afraid he'd give it away. But I didn't want Gabby to get a shot at what I figured he'd expect, the fastball. I was afraid Bill would have trouble getting the curve over or might hang up one in Hartnett's eyes."

Frisch paused. "Walker," he said, "broke off the best curve ball I believe I ever saw. Hartnett took it for strike three to end the game, and the crowd must have thought I was nuts because I stood out there at second base, hands on my knees, head down, as the fans surged onto the field. That's how spent I was."

With six games to go for the Cardinals, four for the Giants, the Redbirds were two behind. That day, as Dizzy Dean won number twenty-eight, beating Pittsburgh, 3-2, the Giants lost to Philadelphia. With Branch Rickey's blessing, and Frank Frisch's annoyance, captain Leo Durocher married a chic dress designer, Grace Dozier. Ernie Orsatti was best man. As Bob Hood recalled, old Hollywood Ern gave it a theatrical touch. He juggled the boxes containing the wedding rings.

A good business woman such as Grace could help straighten out Durocher's fouled-up finances, but she couldn't hit for Lippy Leo. And when the Cardinals were shut out by the old Yankee star, Waite Hoyt, Mrs. Durocher cried. The same day, though, the Giants lost again.

With New York idle, Durocher's wedding began to pay off. The Lip drove in two runs with two hits as the Cardinals beat the Reds, 8-5. Leo was hot the next day, too, as Dizzy shut out Cincinnati, 4-0, tying the race with two games to go.

Now, a winter remark made by Bill Terry at a press conference during a visit to New York for the annual writers' dinner came back to haunt him. Memphis Bill hadn't meant it as a slight, but, aware the Dodgers had done nothing in the trading mart, Terry was asked about the interborough rivals. "Is Brooklyn still in the National League?" he jested.

Classic Confrontation:
Throughout their careers as players and managers, Frank Frisch and Leo Durocher knew the words—and music—to pour into umpires' ears as they do here in a clutch moment of '34.

Meanwhile, J. Roy Stockton thought he'd seen something, and asked third-base coach Mike Gonzalez if he'd seen what he thought he saw. Namely, shortstop Gordon Slade of the Reds relaying battery signs to the outfield so that Cincinnati outfielders could get a jump. You know, a lefthanded hitter is more likely to pull a curve to right field, and a lefthanded batter is more apt to get out in front of a breaking ball and hook it to the left.

"S-h-h," cautioned Gonzalez, furtively, "you do what Mike, she tole you, you forget. Mike, she catch 'em quick. Slade, she hold glove to side on fastball, on knee when curve. Mike, she no tell hitter how, but only what and just enough."

Smart dummy, that smart dummy, Miguel Angel Gonzalez, who was manager Frisch's favorite social partner, along with team surgeon Dr. Robert F. Hyland, owner Preston Bradshaw of the Coronado Hotel, and maybe a blind umpire or two.

So Paul Dean won, 6-1. And when Brooklyn's Van Lingle Mungo beat Hubbell, 5-1, the Cardinals were in first place. St. Louis, which drew only 334,866 in 1934, poured in almost one-third of its home attendance that final week.

Even before the horns could toot, whistles shriek, and rumble-seat convertibles rumble through St. Louis' streets, the Cardinals were pennant-winners. The Giants lost the last day, 8-5, before Dizzy Dean shut out the Reds, 9-0, for victory number thirty. It was the last time a National League pitcher won that many.

As the Cardinals hooted and hollered their way into the clubhouse, Rip Collins sang a Depression song hit, "We're in the Money," and with good reason. The Ripper had been the number one Redbird batsman with a .333 average, thirty-five homers, and 128 runs batted in.

"Buckerinoes, boys, buckerinoes," trainer Harrison J. (Doc) Weaver, mother hen to the Redbirds, beamed with a bastardization of English and Spanish. Yes, winning World Series shares of $5,389.75 would be worth more than a season's salary to several of the "hungry" players Rickey and Breadon liked to keep around.

Breadon could be generous, but tight. He even questioned how much electricity secretary Clarence Lloyd's newfangled clock in the office used. Clarence took the hint and unplugged the electric timepiece.

The electricity was on the special Wabash train that carried the Cardinals to Detroit for the World Series. Frisch's scrapbook contained a specially prepared Redbird-decorated dinner menu from that train. A steak dinner, elegantly supported by all the extras, cost only $1.50.

The Gang was hungover after a private celebration at Jim Mertikas' Grecian Gardens restaurant, formerly located in the downtown, slum-clearance area of St. Louis' Busch Memorial Stadium. Old red-faced Dazzy Vance, the florid-faced Florida philosopher who'd had to wait until nearly forty-four to get into a Series, couldn't find a bartender who knew how to make a "Dazz-Marie."

Vance stepped behind the bar and mixed it himself. He filled an oversized, ice-laden glass with rye, bourbon, Scotch, gin, sloe gin, vermouth, brandy and Benedictine. Then he added powdered sugar, stirred it up, and topped the witch's brew with a cherry. Finding no one with courage enough to join in, Dazzy downed the alcoholic doozy himself.

Detroit, wild over its first pennant since Ty Cobb was a kid in 1909, fielded a team that had won 101 games, seven more than the Cardinals. The G-Men—Charley Gehringer, Hank Greenberg and Goose Goslin—led by Mickey Cochrane, were one-upped by the Cardinals at the outset. The Birds came onto Navin Field as the Tigers were working out the day before the Series.

In street clothes, Dizzy Dean sauntered up to the batting cage, took a bat from startled Greenberg, and said to the future Hall of Fame slugger, "Here, Moe, let me show you how to do it." Diz hit one into the left field bleachers.

The morning of the Series opener, Dizzy and brother Paul were invited to have breakfast with automobile pioneer Henry Ford, the Series radio sponsor. Humorist Will Rogers, an Oklahoman who spoke Dizzy's twang of the Southwest, and Ray Gillespie, young St. Louis writer, were in the automobile as Rogers coached Dean on how to greet the famous man.

At his Dearborn mansion, Ford extended a hand in greeting. "Welcome, Mr. Dean," Mr. Ford said.

Dizzy pumped the old man's hand too vigorously. Rogers winced as the Great One said, "Put 'er there, Henry, I'm sure glad to be here 'cause I heard so much about you, but I'm sorry I'm a-gonna have to make pussycats out of your Tigers."

At the ball park, arriving late, Dizzy put on quite a show. He draped a tiger skin around his gray traveling baseball uniform with the red number "17," amd oompahed into the tuba of a band on the field. Then he proceeded to win the Series opener, 8-3.

At one point he fooled around, pitching to the tall, strong Greenberg. Frisch trotted in from second base. "Dammit, Jerome, quit fooling around," said the Flash, "or I'll yank your butt out of there. Keep the ball down."

Dean was solicitous. "Oh, Frankie," he haw-hawed, "you ain't a-gonna take out Ol' Diz. All these good folks would think you was crazy. I'm just a-figurin' that Moe can't hit my high hard one."

Frisch grumbled his way back to second base. Bang! Greenberg hit the next high fastball out of the park. As the slugger circled the bases, Dean turned to an apoplectic Frisch. "Don't get excited, Frank, 'cause it won't happen again. 'Sides, you're right. Moe can hit the dog-bleep out of a high fast one . . . "

IF YOU wonder why Frisch didn't come right back with brother Paul

Dean in the second game, there were two reasons. For one, the Flash recognized that Bill Hallahan, the sturdy, short southpaw, was a big-game pitcher, as witnessed by his work in 1930 and '31 World Series. Additionally, Frisch thought it would aid the twenty-year-old Paul Dean to let him start before a friendly crowd at home.

Frisch was right, but it turned out wrong. Hallahan pitched brilliantly against towering righthanded Lynwood (Schoolboy) Rowe, who had tied an American League record of sixteen consecutive victories. Schoolie was twitted by St. Louis bench jockeys for having said, "How 'm ah doin', Edna," on a national radio broadcast heard by his fiancee in Arkansas and by those rabbit-eared Redbirds at the Booke-Cadillac Hotel. But he also worked a good game. However, despite a misplay in center field by Orsatti that kept Hallahan from having a shutout, Wild Bill led into the ninth, 2-1.

Then, with one out and a runner in scoring position, DeLancey and Collins permitted a pop foul by Gerald Walker to drop between them. Reprieved, Gee Walker drove in the tying run, and drove out Hallahan. Detroit beat Bill Walker in the twelfth, 3-2. Frisch was fit to be tied as if he were the Old Man (McGraw) he'd helped bury earlier in the year.

"You chowderheads blew the damned ball game for Hallahan," he stormed into the visitors' clubhouse. And then, aware of the presence of the press, he shooed writers angrily out of the clubhouse until the fire of anger had ebbed a bit.

Back home, with Paul Dean opposing little Tommy Bridges of the crackling overhanded curve, Pepper Martin opened with a double off the right field screen. Jack Rothrock tripled. The infield pulled in. Frisch, who'd learned the old Baltimore chop from McGraw, tomahawked

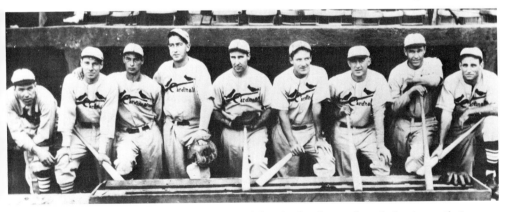

The Gas House Gang: *From right to left, the batting order of the team that opened and closed the 1934 Series at Detroit: Pepper Martin, Jack Rothrock, Frank Frisch, Joe Medwick, Rip Collins, Bill Delancey, Ernie Orsatti, Leo Durocher, and Dizzy Dean.*

downward at a breaking pitch, and bounced it over Gehringer's head at second base for a run-scoring single. Paul Dean had enough to win, 4-1.

By now, the Series was heating up orally and physically. DeLancey had drawn a $50 fine for language unbecoming to the tender ears of veteran American League umpire Brick Owens. Then, Judge Landis, who knew all the words, too, was appalled to learn that Bill Klem, the National League's famed arbiter, and Goose Goslin, Detroit's left field veteran, had exchanged them on a hotel elevator. Another pair of fines. Yep, umpire, too.

With the likes of Pepper Martin diving pell-mell into people, including putting Mickey Cochrane into a hospital overnight, Frisch couldn't complain over retaliating strikes. But a second baseman is fair game even when the foe isn't going out of its way to give him the business. Uncle Frank could remember when he had to tell Dizzy Dean in the midst of an exhibition game at Miami to quit throwing at Terry, because, crissakes, Giants' pitchers retaliated by throwing at the Old Flash.

But the consummate professional, although a bit of a crybaby in his own clubhouse, especially the sanctuary of that morgue-like slab Doc Weaver used as a trainer's table in cramped quarters, Frisch wouldn't complain when Detroit's leadoff man, JoJo White, a base stealing threat, began to bowl over the old pro as if Frankie were the headpin in a bowling alley.

Finally, sympathetically, chesty Leo Durocher watched White knock the props from under those aching legs once again and proposed, "Why not let me cover when we think he's coming down, Frank?"

"No, thanks," said Frisch, then added brightly, "but maybe next time we BOTH can cover."

Bless the Detroit newspaper caption writer who had labeled a photograph of Cochrane "Our Stricken Leader," giving the Cardinals' bench more fodder to fill the Detroit manager's fiery jug ears! The Cardinals' second-base combination gave JoJo White the works—literally—the next time the Detroit outfielder slid into second base. Indeed, Frisch and Durocher both charged over to cover. The Old Flash sat heavily on White's back in unorthodox chiropractic pressure and Lippy Leo sat right on JoJo's head.

But the Series took a turn for the worse—and then some. In the fourth game, won easily by Elden Auker over Tex Carleton and associates, 10-4, St. Louis pitching was sabotaged by three errors by Pepper Martin. Additionally, pinch-running for Spud Davis, Dizzy Dean leaped recklessly, if gallantly, to break up a double play and was conked right on the head by Bill Rogell, the Detroit shortstop.

Dizzy collapsed and was carried off with coach Clyde (Buzzy) Wares clucking soothingly into his ear. Even before X-rays of J. Dean's skull "showed nothing," as the newspaper put it, Paul Dean knew Diz would be all right.

Why?

"Because he was talking."

And saying what?

"Nuthin', just talkin'."

Frisch, criticized for having used the National League's Most Valuable Player so menially, defended his position with what amounted to frankness if not tight-ship leadership. "For one thing," said the Old Flash, "we do have only a twenty-one-man roster, and Spud is slow. For another, Dean is a helluva good athlete, and fast. For a third . . . "

Here Frisch threw up his hands and sighed, "For a third, the hard-playing S.O.B. was down there running himself for Davis."

The next day, insisting on pitching with a headache, Dizzy did all right. But Tommy Bridges did even better, giving up only a homer to Bill DeLancey. Detroit won, 3-1, and headed back to Navin Field needing only one more.

Frisch could have gone with Hallahan, who'd had three days' rest, but he chose Paul Dean, who had only two, and the young righthanded youngster combined with Durocher to win an exciting sixth game from Rowe, 4-3. The shortstop had three hits. The pitcher, himself, drove in the seventh-inning tie-breaker.

The wheels were spinning in Frisch's head even as he walked into the clubhouse, removed his perspiration-soaked sweatshirt, lit a cigarette and untied, then kicked off spiked shoes from his feet, one of which throbbed painfully from that years' old spike wound. He told reporters, seeking his seventh-game starter, "Hallahan" and then deliberately dallied.

Later, Leo Durocher, who would become a long-time, innovative manager with, as Branch Rickey would smile, "a capacity for making a

Bong! Bong!: *The day after shortstop Bill Rogell of Detroit skulled Dizzy Dean with a thrown ball in the 1934 World Series and sent him to the ground and a hospital, the Tiger shortstop presented the Cardinals' pitcher with a World War I helmet.*

bad situation infinitely worse," decided that he had maneuvered Dizzy Dean into the seventh-game showdown, urging Ol' Diz to confront Frisch firmly but fairly.

"Instead," Durocher would say, "Diz slapped the Dutchman on top of the bald spot on his head and said, 'How the hell you a-gonna pitch Hallahan, Frank, when you got Ol' Diz?'"

Frisch would smile at that version. "Good story," he'd say, "but a figment of Leo's fertile imagination. I knew it had to be Dizzy even though I had great respect for Hallahan in a clutch, but Dean had got us that far. He deserved to win or lose it.

"But," the Old Flash emphasized, "I wanted him to want it badly, enough so that he wouldn't sit up and swap stories with Will Rogers or show off with his friends. So I shrugged my shoulders when he exclaimed, 'Hallahan!' and let him follow me late and alone into the showers.

"Before long he was pleading, darn near in tears of anger and frustration, and finally I said to him, 'All right, Jerome, you're going to pitch, but I want you to promise the Old Flash you'll get a good night's sleep because I'll tell you something, my young friend: You win this damned game, and, Depression or not, you'll be able to write your own ticket for $50,000 or more in extras.'"

And so, touching off that big third-inning of the seventh game, Dizzy Dean stretched a single into a double and Frisch knocked out Elden Auker with that clutch three-run double. Dizzy tied a record by getting a second hit that inning. And when they posted a big white "7" on the old-fashioned scoreboard, the Tigers were what Ol' Diz had said they were—pussycats.

Oh, the crowd was unhappy, so distraught that when Joe Medwick tripled for his eleventh Series hit in the sixth inning, tangling with third baseman Marv Owen in a kicking tussle magnified by the mutinous attitude of the sorehead spectators, Medwick trotted out to left field to face a barrage.

J. Roy Stockton called it the "Battle of Produce Row" because not only were empty bottles and box lunches thrown out on the field at number "7," standing there defiantly with hands on hips, but also apple cores, bananas, hardboiled eggs and other items sold by an enterprising vendor out on the street beyond left field. He tossed up to the customers, middle men in the assault on Jersey Joe.

Finally, Durocher came out and put an arm around Medwick and said, "They can't do that to you, Joey. Don't back off."

Snapped Medwick, "If you're so damned brave, why don't you play left field, and let me play shortstop?"

Judge Landis, chin characteristically resting on arms crisscrossed on a boxseat railing, got up at one point in the delay, went back to converse with a man, then returned to his seat. Finally, he summoned Medwick, Frisch, Owen and Mickey Cochrane to his box.

Medwick told the truth. Although the Judge knew that hotheads would

Judgment? Yer Honor's Foot: Frank Frisch threw down his glove in disgust, and Joe Medwick stormed off the field when baseball commissioner K. M. Landis ordered Muscles to take a hike rather than forfeit the seventh game of the 1934 World Series.

be sore losers, Landis didn't want to forfeit a World Series game. He looked out at the 10-0 spread, St. Louis on the scoreboard, and said, "For your own sake, Medwick, you're out of the game."

Frisch exploded, pounding his bare fist into his glove for emphasis, but the commissioner was unflappable. He knew that Frisch knew he wouldn't have taken that kind of action if the game had been close. Nobody scared Kenesaw Mountain Landis, named for a Civil War battle near Chattanooga.

The Old Flash didn't like it, especially when replacement Chick Fullis got the twelfth hit that Medwick might have achieved to tie the then-existing record for Series safeties. The Hungarian Rhapsody would be given a protective police escort back to the hotel after the 11-0 rout, and a couple of Detroit detectives would eat dinner with him and roommate Hallahan in their rooms, until time to catch a midnight sleeper back to St. Louis.

Meanwhile, Dizzy Dean had been holding forth. "Well, I'll be dawg-goned," he said, grinning, "at times I just don't know how good me 'n Paul are. Imagine, back there in the spring when I said the Dean boys would win forty-five games, and none of you people would believe me. For pity sake, I didn't even know myself then how good we were."

They'd won fifty-three. Count 'em. Thirty for Dizzy, nineteen for Paul, a forty-nine total in the regular season, and two each in the World Series.

"Hey, Mr. DeWitt, where's those endorsements you want Ol' Diz to sign?"

Frankie Frisch laughed. The reluctant dragon bit had worked and, besides, the Old Flash's sturdy football-developed chest was puffed out over that game-breaking blow off Auker.

"I'd rather have had that base-clearing hit when the game was on the line than to have hit .800," said Frank Francis Frisch, inclined at times to exaggerate. But he probably was not stretching that fact in the climax-capping highlight of a year in which he'd even called his shot in the All-Star game at the Polo Grounds. There, he called a shot, hitting a leadoff home run into the upper right field deck off the Yankees' Lefty Gomez.

But Warren Brown, Chicago writer, had heard the Old Flash before, shrinking or shrieking. What, Brownie wondered, had Judge Landis been doing back there talking a few rows behind his Detroit boxseat at the Medwick onslaught? Surely a great jurist hadn't needed legal advice? Maybe police counsel about crowd control?

The Judge laughed. "No, Warren," he said, "and don't write this, but for years I've been trying to learn how to spit tobacco through my teeth. And, waiting for the crowd to calm down, I'd watched Pepper Martin do it. He's absolutely marvelous at squirting a straight stream, not at all messy, and by jove, suddenly I had it.

"I just couldn't resist rushing back and telling a friend of mine. Watch!"

Pa-tooie!

Calling His Shot: Before the 1934 All-Star game at New York's Polo Grounds, Frank Frisch told a St. Louis writer that if the Yankees' Lefty Gomez grooved the first pitch, the Flash would hit a home run. Righthanded, Uncle Frank hit the upper right field seats, and is congratulated by Pittsburgh's Pie Traynor as he scores.

17

The Gang Runs
Out of Gas

DAWGONNIT," said Paul Dean, forty-five years and more than 100 pounds later, "if 'Dutch' hadn't got hurt early, and Terry Moore late, we'd won the next year, too. We wuz a better ball club in 1935—and won more games."

Indeed, as Dizzy's younger brother, a silver-haired, over-stuffed senior citizen from Springdale, Arkansas, put it as the 1970s were slipping off the calendar, Frankie Frisch's "Cawd-nuls" were better the year they officially became the Gas House Gang than they were as world champions in 1934.

Although that famous Gas House nickname was one of the best-known ever in sports, its antecedents are annoyingly inexact. For instance, witty Warren Brown, acerbic Chicago sports writer, felt he'd hung it on the Cardinals as far back as 1932 or '33. A result, Warren would say, of Pepper Martin in general, and one of the Wild Horse's knock-'em-dead-and-let-'em-lay antics in particular. Or maybe just the way Johnny looked in uniform, like the good-natured, train-hopping hobo he'd been when he had the financial shorts, and a long way to go.

Appearance did indeed play a part in talented Frank Graham's description in the old *New York Sun.* Maybe it was earlier than research, or just eluded Frisch's own scrapbooks in the Hall of Fame library at Cooperstown, New York. But, coincidentally, the "Gas House Gang" wasn't used in St. Louis by J. Roy Stockton of *The Post-Dispatch* until August, 1935. At the time, charging to the fore as in the past, the Redbirds were in the East on a handsome fourteen-game winning streak.

From New York, where Frisch's merry men of mischief had mixed it, and won a pivotal series from Bill Terry's Giants, catching New York earlier than in '34, Stockton wrote that the press in the Big Apple had called the colorful cutthroats aptly "the Gas House Gang." That seemed to coincide with the heat of the summer, the pennant race and apparently with Graham's twitching-eared memory for a quote.

Walking toward him with gray road uniforms, dirty from a hot series in Boston—the players averaged only about a uniform and a half then, and clubhouses had no dry-cleaning facilities—was a long line of crumby bums. They trooped into the visiting team's third-base dugout at New York's Polo Grounds for a Sunday doubleheader, led by Graham's New Rochelle neighbor, Frank Frisch.

Uncle Frank never worried about how he looked. Whether his sweatshirt sleeve was tattered, and the uniform was almost as grimy as Pepper Martin's, it didn't matter as long as his sanitary white stockings were clean, and the half-dozen pairs of baseball shoes he wore a season were shined. Trainer Doc Weaver, one of Frank's favorites, who also had joined the Cardinals in 1927, had always hammered the importance of taking care of the feet. With that old throbbing spike wound, the Flash believed him.

Pitcher Bill Walker fit the description of "stylish," on and off the field, but the neatest regular, even in the baggy flannels of the period, was the slick shortstop, Leo Durocher. And when Graham made some reference to the American League race, Dizzy Dean scoffed, and said, "Heck, they wouldn't even let us play over in that lollipop league."

Durocher, with a voice that could break the sound barriers, rasped, "That's right. They don't want any Gas Housers over there."

So Graham, his fingers typing what his eyes had seen and his ears had heard, made reference to the "Gas House Gang." But was that the first time, the late summer of '35? Frisch's Cooperstown scrapbook shows that on May 14, Willard Mullin, gifted sports cartoonist of *The New York World-Telegram,* had used a Gas House sketch to illustrate a story, written by puckish Tom Meany, of a game in which Durocher hit a tenth-inning homer to beat the Giants, 3-2.

Meany wrote, in part, "Those Cardinals of his [Frisch] are still baseball's Gas House Gang—rough, rowdy, and ready . . . "

The best version, whether it was first, second, third, or last, occurred after an extra-inning game was won by the Cardinals from the Cubs on July 4, at a packed house in Chicago's Wrigley Field. With Pepper Martin on third, Ernie Orsatti on second, Burgess Whitehead grounded to shortstop Bill Jurges, who fumbled momentarily, then threw to the plate to head off the leading run.

The ball and Pepper arrived at the same time. Catcher Ken O'Dea went one way in the collision, the ball in another, and the Wild Horse was safe. Orsatti, rounding third, followed. When O'Dea got up, he retrieved the ball and threw to pitcher Lon Warneke, covering home. Orsatti barreled into the tall, slender Arkansas Hummingbird, and Warneke went galley west.

THE CARDINALS swept the holiday second game, too. If anyone had said then that Charley Grimm's Cubs would win the pennant, he or she would have been as sheepish as the Cubbies must have been that night, headed east by train, when Warren Brown walked through their quiet Pullman cars.

"What's the matter?" Brownie teased. "You boys afraid that Pepper Martin is on the train? Better stay on your side of the tracks or the Gas House Gang will get you."

But the Cubs had the last laugh in 1935. From Labor Day on, they went on a spectacular twenty-one-game winning streak and, although the Cardinals traditionally played well in September, the Cubs went by the Giants and then even the Gas House Gang.

As Paul Dean put it, the 1935 version of the Gang was stronger. Dizzy had won twenty-eight games, and Paul had repeated his nineteen. They sliced up some $150,000 in "extras" that Bill DeWitt had lined up after the 1934 World Series. The Cardinals' treasurer corralled endorsements, personal appearances, barnstorming and more that he lined up into '35 as their agent.

Cripes, Frisch had been conservative when he told Dizzy what winning that final game in the '34 Series might mean at a time when silver dollars looked as big as manhole covers.

"I liked Dutch," said Paul Dean, describing for the manager. "He'd been a great player who was still good in a pinch, and, partly because of Ray Blades' experience with me at Columbus and Mike Gonzalez's encouragement, he stayed with me in 1934."

As Dizzy's younger brother said, winning ninety-six games to ninety-five the year before, the Cardinals were a bit better in 1935, a season for which Dizzy held out to get his salary doubled to $15,000, and Paul was increased from $3,000 to $7,500. Joe Medwick was devastating with .354 average, 126 RBIs and eighty-nine extra-base hits among his 224. Bill Hallahan, the lefthanded veteran, bounced back with a fifteen-game season.

Handsome, curly-haired Terry Moore, a home-town rookie put into center field, was spectacular defensively and a surprising .287 hitter for a first-year man. Down the stretch, the youngest player, Moore, just twenty-three, and Frisch, reaching thirty-eight, carried the club.

The Old Flash, playing only 103 games, had been out too long, a result of a nasty gash at the heel of his gloved hand, suffered from the sliding spikes of Pittsburgh's Gus Suhr. Burgess Whitehead was just what Stockton had nicknamed the graceful second baseman; Whitey was the Gazelle. But he couldn't hit like the old man. In September, when points come hard, even for a reduced-schedule player like the Frisch of 1935, Uncle Frank hiked his average from .260 to .294.

In September, however, after the brothers Dean had avenged the Labor Day doubleheader loss at Pittsburgh the previous year by winning a pair that made it look as if Sam Breadon would have the nation's sports writers as his October guests, the Cubs got incredibly hot, and the Cardinals suffered a crippling loss. Sliding into home plate, Terry Moore broke a leg. An aging Orsatti, returned to center field, immediately misplayed a decisive ball that Terry would have caught with his tooth-paste-ad choppers.

So it came down to a season-ending five-game series, one in which Jolly Cholly Grimm's Cubs needed only two to clinch in the manager's home town. The first one was classic. The Cubs' kid first baseman, Phil Cararretta, hit one to the pavilion roof off Paul Dean, hooked up in a dandy duel with Warneke.

Although not nearly so boisterous as Dizzy, Paul ranted, "Come on, you buzzards, or do I have to hit TWO home runs myself?"

Final score: Chicago 1, St. Louis 0.

It was cold, rainy and raw the next afternoon. That late September day in 1935, with the national American Legion convention in St. Louis, the Gas House Gang expired as champions. The old man, Frisch, got a couple of hits off Bill Leo, to give Dizzy an early lead, but neither Frank nor his pitcher noticed something.

Frisch's teen-age teammate of the 1924 World Series, Chicago's Freddie Lindstrom, although ready to retire prematurely with a bad back, altered his unorthodox double-step stride into the ball, which ordinarily made him vulnerable to inside pitches.

Lindy ripped one, and next time up too. When he came up later, seeking his fourth hit, Frisch yelled impatiently from second base to Dean, "Damnit, I said, 'Pitch him tight.'"

"I am, Frank, but it ain't working," Dizzy hissed.

The Cubs' 6-2 victory clinched the pennant that sent them into a World Series, lost to Detroit in six games. And, after the Cubbies wrapped up a lineup of rinkydink Redbird rookies in the second game that crepe-clinching day in September, Frisch walked out somberly and late, accompanied by his good man Friday, coach Mike Gonzalez.

The canny Cuban couldn't cheer him up, even with his meaningful philosophy, "Nobody die for you, but you, Frohnk." It wouldn't have helped, even as it had one morning at the Coronado, when, after a hungover Frisch overslept, Mike rang his suite and came up, at the manager's request, to order room service.

While shaving, Frisch could hear Gonzalez repeating an item that perplexed the room-service operator. He couldn't fathom the fractured-English version of "sakarakah juss" for "sauerkraut juice." With the Old Flash grinning around his shaving cream, Mike dutifully tried one last time.

"Hokay, I give it you wance more! Sakarakah juss, you catch him? Two fry egg, two-three slice hang, toast, coffee. What? How many time must I tole you? Sakarakah juss . . . sakarakah juss . . . oh, hell, make it orange juss."

Frank Frisch loved to laugh, but only at the right time and in the right place. "He was a hard loser," recalled Terry Moore, "and I just wish I'd played with him when he was younger because the old man could still hit, even when he couldn't move too well. From him and Jesse Haines, I learned as a rookie how serious this game was.

"I'll never forget one game at Cincinnati's Crosley Field, Pop Haines, past forty, looked as if he'd lose because of errors we made behind him. The old guy walked into the old frame visitors' clubhouse, tore out that pot-bellied stove, grinding his teeth. And when we came in after winning it for him, you never saw such a sheepish-looking man, like a kid caught with his hand in the candy jar."

Moore, who captained world championship ball clubs for the Cardinals in 1942 and '46, before and after military service, said he'd learned from the Gas House Gang—and from 1935.

"Seeing a club play so well and still lose, and then finishing second again in 1936, '39 and '41, I never let up on players, even guys like Enos Slaughter, Stan Musial, Marty Marion, Harry Walker and the Coopers [Mort and Walker]. I'd become one of Frisch's hard losers, too. Second place is for the birds—and I don't mean Redbirds."

In 1936, after Branch Rickey was convinced that Whitehead was too frail to stand up to the day-in, day-out strain of daily play, Frisch's heir apparent at second base was dealt to New York. There, Whitey played every game for Bill Terry's team, which did not blow first place either in '36 or '37, a season when the Gazelle missed just two games. Only then did Whitehead cave in.

Not, however, before facing old teammate Dizzy Dean in the sluggish dog days of August at St. Louis. Dean always saw to it that he grooved at least one fat pitch for a personal favorite. Whitey lined a hot shot back through the mound. Old Diz hadn't completed his follow-through when the ball glanced off the side of his head and arched on the fly all the way down to the bullpen for a double. In what seemed slow motion, the Great Dean kept turning until he wound up, seated crosslegged and facing second base, like a lanky Indian puffing a peace pipe.

The brothers Dean and Pepper Martin's musical depreciation had Frisch pulling out his thinning locks. "Pablo," re Paul Dean by Mike Gonzalez, held out for $1,000 to $8,500, and finally signed as the Cardinals broke camp to head north on dastardly one-night, tank-town stands by Pullman. Overweight, Paul had shin splints, but he wanted the ball. He knew, too, that if he weren't ready to pitch, the ball club would dock him. Parenthetically, he always did like the evangelistic Rickey, whose religious zeal more closely matched his own biblical beliefs, than he did club owner Sam Breadon.

"Naw," said Paul Dean, answering a question, "it [trouble] wasn't Dutch's fault. Heck, after Dizzy got knocked out by the Cubs on opening day [1936], I beat Bill Lee the next day, 3-2, and Frisch won it for me with an eighth-inning home run."

By mid-May "at the latest," Paul Dean had won five games, and was rolling along. He pitched nine innings one day, then went in to relieve the next game, which stretched into extra innings. He felt something snap while throwing. From then until 1943, trying on and off, Paul won only a stinking dozen more big league ball games. Ultimately, he operated two filling stations in Springdale, Arkansas, before doing promotion work for A. Ray Smith, Tulsa oil man who operated a nomadic Triple-A franchise with a St. Louis working agreement.

Serenely, Paul Dean blamed no one other than himself for his short career. "Not overwork," he emphasized, "not proper condition. I'd let myself get up to 225 pounds."

Brother Dizzy, ultimately close to the 300 pounds Paul reached later, also had his own troubles as things went from bad to worse for the Cardinals and for the old Dutchman, Frisch. Frankie played only ninety-four games, hitting just .274, and would have played fewer than that if his reed-like replacement, Stu Martin, hadn't come up ailing.

So it didn't matter that the mighty Medwick had battered in 138 runs with ninety-five extra-base blows among 223 hits, sixty-four of them a

"M" Is for Mize: Big Johnny Mize strokes a line drive for the Cardinals, en route to homer-hitting and batting-average brilliance.

record for doubles. It helped, but not enough, that Cincinnati had turned down a provisional deal for a giant, florid-faced first baseman named Johnny Mize, fearful that Branch Rickey had fleeced them because Mize reported with a disabling growth in the groin. Heck, Judge Landis hadn't called Dr. Robert F. Hyland the "surgeon-general of baseball" for nothing.

Frisch's friend and St. Louis social acquaintance put his skilled scalpel to work, and—voila!—Mize began a career that would carry him to the city's still-existing home-run record of forty-three (1940). And later at New York, where he would win honors and ball games as the Big Cat, he homered fifty-one times for the Giants. He was a better pinch-hitter than first baseman with championship Yankee ball clubs.

Watching Mize when Johnny was just an over-grown boy, Casey Stengel, then with Boston and later his boss in the Bronx, described him best. Of Muscles Medwick's other half of the murderous middle of St. Louis's batting order, Old Case said:

"That feller Mize is a slugger who hits like a leadoff man. Pitch him away, and he'll line one to left field. Pitch him inside, and he'll take you on a streetcar ride downtown."

Streetcars went places, farther than the Cardinals or, at times, the Gas House Gang's base-runners. When the Gang stopped off at Cleveland for an exhibition, where the Indians warmed up a nervous, foot-in-the-face, high-kicking kid named Bob Feller that day, Frank Frisch watched as a fast ball whizzed past the warmup catcher and thudded into the backstop.

Frank was a wise old bird. And rank does have its privileges. Frisch beckoned to reserve outfielder Lynn King and said, "Ever play second base?"

"No, Frank."

"Well, you are today."

After Feller fanned eight batters in three innings, Frisch knew why he'd been safer in the dugout. And it was on the bench back at the Polo Grounds, where he'd seen John McGraw writhe over messed-up plays, that he saw the worst since Brooklyn's Babe Herman tripled into a double play.

A pass-in-the-night pitcher, Cotton Pippen, was running the bases at second for the Cardinals. Swift Terry Moore was on first when Art Garibaldi, sawed-off third baseman, shot one to right center. To himself, Tee Moore figured triple, and let out at full speed. He let out so fast that he didn't realize that Mike Gonzalez, coaching third base, sought to play it safe.

"You go," warbled the Senor to Pippen, passing him at third, "he stay."

Pippen, who hadn't majored in either base-running or Spanish, much less the Gonzalez School of English, heard the second part, intended for Moore. He stopped and retreated toward third, compelling Moore to put on the brakes, and head back from third to second. Before Frank Frisch could throw a fit, or his cap, Pippen had been retired in withdrawal at third, and Moore was caught sliding back into second. Garibaldi, who had rounded second, returned to first base. So a possible two-run double or triple had become a two-out single.

When a boiling-mad Moore reached the dugout, Frisch had laid out four towels to simulate bases. The manager opened his mouth to launch a tirade about meatheaded base-running.

Moore kicked one towel into the Flash's face, another onto the dugout roof, and . . .

What did Frisch say?

"Not a damned word," remembered Moore, smiling, "because he could see how hot I was."

At Boston, where Dizzy Dean battled for one of his twenty-four victories, the Cardinals led into the ninth inning, 2-1, two out. The tying run was on second when Vince DiMaggio, oldest of the three baseball brothers, came to the plate. Vince had struck out three times, and now he lifted a high foul behind Bruce Ogrodowski, a kid catcher trying to replace tuberculosis victim Bill DeLancey.

Frisch, seated on the bench, prepared to get to his feet with the joy of victory when he was startled to see Dean rush down toward the plate, hands cupped around his mouth, shouting.

"Drop it, dammit, drop it. If you want to catch me again, drop it . . ."

Surprised, confused, Ogrodowski parted his hands, and the ball fell foul, giving DiMaggio another chance. Frisch hit the ceiling, literally. He leaped and conked his head on the concrete dugout roof. He fell back dazed as Dizzy got the ball back and "fogged," to use his favorite fast-ball verb, a game-ending strike three past the eldest DiMag.

Frisch, enraged, head throbbing from anger as well as pain, wondered what the four-letter word Dean had been doing? Dizzy laughed.

"Take it easy, Frank," Dean was soothing. "Heck, Ol' Diz knew he could strike out that DiMaggio four times any day, and on the train ride over here from New York I bet Johnny Perkins (East St. Louis comedian) that I'd do it. He said I couldn't, so we bet two bits a try and, hell, Frank, you know Ol' Diz ain't a-gonna lose no bets."

But Ol' Diz lost the season-ending game in the rain to the Cubs and Lon Warneke, at St. Louis, 6-3, permitting Chicago to tie the Cardinals for second place behind the Giants with an 87-67 record. The final game was noteworthy because, with Rip Collins hurt, and Johnny Mize ejected, the guy who played the last couple of innings at first base for the first, and only time in the majors, was a rookie named Walter Alston. The man who later managed the Dodgers for twenty-three seasons batted once, struck out, and had only two fielding chances, muffing one.

Before 1937, Dizzy Dean held out, finally wheedling a $25,500 con-tract. Words were exchanged before Branch Rickey appeared late one night at the Deans' home in Bradenton, Florida. B.R. came with smooth words intended to soothe a seething situation. With Dizzy, the wizard of words succeded. But his wife, Pat, snapped uncivilly about the late-night intrusion.

"Oh, Mr. Rickey, she don't mean it," said Ol' Diz.

"The hell I don't," said Pat, a past master at saying what she meant plainly. "He's a stinker."

Frank Frisch must have felt similarly when he saw a quote by Rickey in *The Sporting News*. The general manager had been quoted as saying that he thought the Cardinals had a chance for the 1937 pennant if Frisch, the manager, didn't insist on playing second base. Yet Rickey thought Rogers Hornsby could be blunt!

To bolster Redbird pitching, thinned out by Paul Dean's career-crippling injury, and the athletic demise of lefthanded Bill Hallahan and Bill Walker, Rickey dealt Rip Collins to the Cubs for Lon Warneke, giving Johnny Mize complete control at first base. Also acquired was lefthanded White Sox pitcher, Bob Weiland.

Warneke, Weiland and Frenchy Bordagary, former daffiness Dodger outfielder at Brooklyn under Casey Stengel, served merely to flesh out, and formalize, what became known as Pepper Martin's Mudcats. Called Mississippi Mudcats, or Missouri Mudcats, they'd create cacophony compared with Spike Jones' later organized disorder, chamber music by contrast.

There always had been a loosey-goosey atmosphere around the Redbirds' clubhouse, partly because Doc Weaver, the trainer who favored Hollywood director neck scarves, breezy hats and Rube Goldberg inventions, provided pre-game and post-game music on a record player. After WINNING games only, that is. Judas Priest, as Bucko Weaver's old college football coach, Branch Rickey, would say, the Dutchman would blow his stack if anyone so much as smiled after a lost game.

But Martin, the king of cutups with Dean, the clown prince of the same, began to play his guitar, pronounced "git-tar," and a harmonica. Warneke plunked a guitar, also. Weiland oompahed on a whiskey jug, Bordagaray could make a washboard talk, and Fiddler Bill McGee, a pleasant pitcher, often played the violin more successfully than he pitched.

Did the tail wag the dog? Probably not, but if there had been television then, and the wide array of variety acts and talk shows, money Martin, and his Mudcats, would have made mucho buckerinoes. As it was, they bought cowboy uniforms, and picked up an interesting piece of change here and there on radio programs and theaters, aside from amusing themselves, and annoying Frisch. The Flash could stomach "Birmingham Jail," "Buffalo Gal" and "Possum Up a Gum Stump" after a game that was won. But he'd grumble to himself, growl to Mike Gonzalez or to traveling secretaries Clarence Lloyd or Leo Ward in his railroad drawing room when the Mudcats practiced. Damn, to ears that appreciated Wagner, and would admire the professional ripples of concert pianist Eugene Istomin, that early-version country-western or mournful mountain music of Martin's was sheer nonsense.

THE OLD FLASH played little in 1937, his dogs barking, legs aching. Yes, and as he related in spring training, even the batting eye—the reflexes—were beginning to go, too. Besides, he liked the spunk and spirit of Jimmy Brown, a switch-hitting lad who reminded him of a younger Frisch, in spirit if not ability.

So he not only benched himself, but also Leo Durocher, whose batting average had shrunk. He used Brown and Stu Martin on either side of second base. Then, with the Cardinals slumping, he switched one day at Philadelphia's Baker Bowl. The old double-play team of Durocher and Frisch returned to the lineup. The Old Flash, nearly forty, did so well, and the ball club won so handily the first day that he tried again the next afternoon.

Mind you, this was Baker Bowl, where the right field fence was only 270 feet from the plate at the foul pole. Frisch was the runner at second base, Terry Moore was on first when Joe Medwick's black bat pickled a pitch into the rightfield corner. By the time Frisch's old legs reached third, the fast Moore was rounding second, and Frisch didn't know whether to laugh or cry as he heard Gonzalez exhort him as third-base coach.''

"He come, Frohnk, you go; he come, you go . . . ''

Just as Frisch's spiked shoes touched home plate, his legs were taken out from under him by Moore's slide on Medwick's two-run double. Frisch sat there in tandem with Moore as if back on the bobsled run at Lake Placid. Then he got up, huffing, dusted himself off, and said to Moore:

"What 'n hell did you do? Cut across the pitcher's mound?"

Nearing the bench, Frisch said loudly, "Any time they can run down the Old Flash, it's time to quit. Brown, you go to second base!"

So Frank Frisch hung up his glove before mid-season, 1937. He coached occasionally at third base, where a couple of months later he happened to be when the Cardinals played Bill McKechnie's Boston Braves at St. Louis. The Redbirds were going no place, which fourth place (81-73) represented to a constant contender. It was a midweek game with few of the paying faithful on hand.

Trailing a run, bases loaded in the ninth inning, two out, Frisch looked into the dugout for a pinch-hitter to bat for young catcher Mickey Owen. From the shadows of the enclave, a voice disguised in falsetto yelled.

"Why don't you hit, GRANDMA?"

Frank Frisch's neck reddened. The old competitive fire flared. The Old Flash walked over to the batrack, picked up a stick, walked up to the plate, announced himself properly to the umpire, and then waited patiently as McKechnie made a pitching change to bring in his best reliever, Milkman Jim Turner. Then, Frisch slapped Turner's first pitch on a sharp high hop over first baseman Elbie Fletcher's head into right field. The tying run scored. The winning run followed (6-5), and you would have thought that Frisch had won another big one for the old

Gang. Led by Pepper Martin, they rushed down to first base to pick up the old Dutchman or, at least, try to. He had one leg on the ground, one hoisted in the air, as Pepper strong-armed the grinning field foreman to the bench.

It would have been nice—poetic justice, symbolic—if Frank Francis Frisch had made his last time at bat in the majors a game-winning basehit. But how many of the great ones go out on top? Did Babe Ruth doff his cap and disappear in 1935 when, out of sheer memory, he hit three home runs at Pittsburgh; long, longer, and l-o-n-g-e-s-t?

Frisch tried once more, the very next day in 1937, in fact, against Boston's bespectacled Danny MacFayden. It looked as if the Old Flash had come through again. He hit one sharply past the pitcher and over second base, but Boston's shortstop, Rabbit Warstler, had been playing Uncle Frank as if he were the mind-reading Old Flash himself. He was close enough to the bag and made the play, gloving the ground ball, stepping on second and then firing to first base. Doubled up as he tried to let out, Frisch pulled a leg muscle and hobbled off, lame and defeated.

So ended the nineteen-year career of Frankie Frisch, who, fresh off the college campus, went right from Fordham's Rose Hill to New York's Polo Grounds, and to stardom. A career batting average of .316, dragged down those last few seasons, including an embarrassing .219 for only thirty-two times up in 1937, did not illustrate his effectiveness with a bat in his hand. And even though, at times, he committed the fewest errors at his position, fielding figures do not tell the tale of either the Flash's defensive range or spectacular play. His base-running was breath-taking. He merited his Hall of Fame election in 1947, a decade after he retired, when he was selected for Cooperstown with extremely good company—pitcher Carl Hubbell, catcher Mickey Cochrane and third baseman Pie Traynor.

As a manager, Frisch lost considerably when Dizzy Dean, of whom he was so genuinely fond, was hurt immediately after the 1937 All-Star game. Typically, Ol' Diz had tried to duck it. "Naively," he followed his luggage to St. Louis, but Sam Breadon and wife Pat prevailed on Dean to go to Washington. At a time baseball people just didn't fly, Breadon himself flew to D.C. with Dizzy. There, presumably facing his last man of what could have been a successful three-inning stint, Dean was hit on the left big toe by a line drive smashed by Cleveland's Earl Averill.

The toe was broken, a splint fashioned. Dr. Hyland advised rest, but, shucks, the Cardinals needed Ol' Diz—in his judgment as well as theirs—and within ten days he was in Boston, where he told Frisch that, podnuh, he was ready.

Of course, Frisch made a mistake in using him. Bill McKechnie, coaching third base for his Braves, watched Dean warm up unnaturally, favoring the tender toe.

"Don't, Jerome, don't," he warned.

But Jerome, or rather, Jay did. He was going along fine when, suddenly, pitching in a late inning against Bill Urbanski, something snapped in his right shoulder, which dangled, as McKechnie, a compassionate man, wailed.

"I told you, Jerome, I told you . . . "

On the eve of the 1938 season Dizzy Dean was traded as damaged goods to Chicago for $185,000 and three ball players. Pitchers Curt Davis and Clyde Shoun would help the Cardinals subsequently, but Philip K. Wrigley, the sportsman who owned the Cubs, then active at the ball park before becoming a Howard Hughes of baseball, never complained.

"Having Dizzy Dean was like traveling with a brass band," reminisced Wrigley, years later, "and he not only drew well, but in limited appearances, he did help us win the 1938 pennant."

The day before manager Gabby Hartnett's homer in the gloaming gave the Cubs the edge over rival Pittsburgh, an ailing-armed Dean came off the shelf and slow-curved Chicago to a 2-1 victory, giving him seven victories out of eight that season. The first had been a masterful slowball performance, shutting out Frisch's Cardinals before a standing-room only crowd at Wrigley Field in April.

Terry Moore, who doubled twice for half of the four shutout hits off Dizzy, said he knew it would be a long season when Rickey, who loved experiments, had set up a special camp at Winter Haven, Florida, before the opening of spring training at St. Petersburg, the Cardinals' winter quarters ever since.

B.R. wanted Frisch to try Moore, the center field master, at third base; third baseman Don Gutteridge at shortstop, and outfielder Don Padgett as a catcher. Frisch, teaching kids how to slide, chipped an ankle bone.

"And," said Moore, "I remember at a pre-season dinner, when Rickey told the St. Louis crowd with a straight face, 'Except for pitching, this is the best ball club the Cardinals have ever fielded.'"

Moore smiled, "I nudged the player next to me and said, 'Oh, oh, it won't be long for the Flash . . . ' "

Terry's Irish grin broadened. "Ah, Uncle Frank," he said, fondly, "I didn't have to hit too much to suit him because he recognized the need for defense in key positions. But he stayed with me my second and third years when I was trying to pull outside pitches, popping weakly to third and short. He'd say, 'Dammit, Terry, you've got to go to right field.'

"So he's managing at Pittsburgh a couple of years later, and I hit-and-run beautifully into right field for a basehit. And as I got down to first base, I yelled to him at the Pittsburgh bench, 'Hey, Frank, I got it, I got it.' "

"He waved at me, disgustedly, but I think, a little proud, too," he said.

In 1938, when the Cardinals went to Rochester for an exhibition game, billboards and handbills proclaimed in large type, "PEPPER MARTIN

AND HIS MUDCATS HERE.'' Smaller type added ''Also, the Cardinals with Joe Medwick and Johnny Mize.''

Medwick growled, ''What the bleep is this: A ball club or a band?''

Back in St. Louis, pleading for relief provided by Breadon via Rickey to Martin, Frisch was at his whining, nasal best to get the Mudcats disbanded.

''Mr. Breadon,'' the Flash pleaded, ''Mr. Breadon, I'm the only manager required to travel with an or-CHES-tra.''

Or-CHES-tra was, of course, a high-rent district description for low-down noisemakers.

In September, with the Cardinals sixth, Breadon called Frisch in and, choking back the tears, Singin' Sam told his favorite player that he felt the time had come for a managerial change after five-plus seasons.

''Don't feel bad about it, Mr. Breadon,'' said Frisch, trying to help, tears in his eyes as he headed back to New York and to dear Ada and their English-style horticulturist's delight on New Rochelle's Fenimore Road.

Missouri Mudcats: *Pepper Martin's masters of musical depreciation even dressed the part. Stanley (Frenchy) Bordaray squats in front with a washboard. From the left, Lon Warneke, guitar; Bill McGee, violin; Max Lanier, harmonica; and Pepper, guitar.*

A year later, trying the elocutionist patience of Harvard's public-speaking department, Frisch was in Boston, a battler replacing popular Fred Hoey as play-by-play broadcaster of the big league ball clubs' home games. He liked the fresh seafood even better, and the chance to golf, a game at which the great all-round athlete did not excel.

When he was living it up on the seashore near Boston, he was offered the job as manager at New Orleans. The figure, $12,000 in 1940, was a pretty good one. It meant the thrill of putting on the monkey suit again and getting down into the pits.

The Braves' club president, venerable Bob Quinn, put it straight for him. "Listen, Frank," he said, "New Orleans is a fine city, good tourist town, but that's still minor-league ball, and you've never lived or traveled under minor-league conditions."

Frisch turned down the Pelicans with thanks, and was rewarded the next year with a contract succeeding Pie Traynor at Pittsburgh. In seven years with the Benswangers, heirs to baseball pioneer Barney Dreyfus, he came close once, finishing second to the "Cawd'nuls" in 1944. By then, Rickey had left St. Louis a Comstock legacy of home-grown, farm-system talent. In 1938, the year B.R. had encouraged Breadon to can his pet, the Old Flash, Rickey had been accused by Judge Landis of covering up ninety-one farm-system players. In fairness to B.R., the man who at Brooklyn gave the black man that long-overdue chance, a salary-bonus arrangement totaling $80,000 didn't help Rickey's position. Breadon also had constant concern about each season's bucks—especially with war clouds gathering.

Once, although Breadon would have preferred to move the colorful Cardinals to Detroit if the American League Tigers had been foolish enough to move over to make room, a Ponca City, Oklahoma, oil man named Lew Wentz evinced interest in buying the Redbirds. Then Wentz shilly-shallied. Finally, Breadon pulled his watch like an old-fashioned umpire, and said he'd give the prospective purchaser a half-hour longer.

Thirty minutes later, as cold as his blue eyes when he felt he'd been led astray, Breadon said, "Time's up, Mr. Wentz, good day."

Visiting St. Louis with the Pirates, Frisch would drop in to see Breadon, and to break bread with Dr. Bob Hyland. He'd spend time in St. Louis or Pittsburgh with the Redbird traveling secretary he'd broken in late in 1937, Leo Ward. He'd taught Ward an important lesson.

Dining one night in Boston with the young road nursemaid to the Cardinals, he'd casually mentioned the ball club's railroad tickets, some $4,000 worth, certain that Ward had locked them up. The startled sec said, my gosh, no, he'd left them in the suite.

"All right, cement head, calm down," said the Flash, after getting his message across, "I hid them under the mattress, but let that be a lesson."

Naturally, too, Frisch would find time to visit with the man who had nursed his lumbago, and other injuries, real or imagined, Doc Weaver, the trainer. In 1938, Frisch's last year as St. Louis manager, landlubber Frisch and nautical Weaver had bought a 48-foot rumrummer in Boston, and accompanied by their wives, had taken the inland water route from New York to Florida.

"A bloody disaster," Frisch recalled. "We damn near capsized in Chesapeake Bay and had engine trouble near Norfolk. A trip that was supposed to take about a week lasted three weeks, and when we got to Florida, I said, 'Doc, you've got a present—my half of the boat.'"

Frisch had a way of becoming close with off-the-field friends of his various baseball families, such as the New York Giants' legendary Eddie Brannick, Pittsburgh's traveling secretary, Bob Rice and the Chicago Cub's rotund Bob Lewis.

Rice, a former ball player and manager in the minors, remembered how the Flash had cackled with glee in by-play after Rice was stricken with appendicitis on the desert near Pittsburgh's former spring-training site at San Bernardino, California. Solicitously, Frisch leaped into the ambulance that whisked the moaning secretary to a designated hospital, only to chortle when the siren-sounding ambulance drove up to find a sign that read:

"For Sale—Hospital."

F RISCH'S expressed regret when taking over at Pittsburgh was that the Waner brothers, Paul and Lloyd, were not the devastating hitters he had known for years in St. Louis.

The Flash said, "Stengel would say that Paul was such an artful slider, he wouldn't break a bottle in his hip pocket. All I know is that when Dizzy [Dean] was at his best, and could strike out Bill Terry as if he were a 'sem-eye' pro, Paul Waner hit as if he owned him.

Right Players, Wrong Time: *Frank Frisch, taking over as Pittsburgh manager in 1940, is welcomed by two long-time Pirate stars who had bedeviled the Cardinals, Lloyd Waner and Paul Waner. The veteran outfielders were soon to be dealt by the Bucs.*

"One day Paul was so hungover at game time that the fumes were coming off, and his eyes were slits. All he did was to tag Dean for four doubles, tying the record."

When the Pirates were sold near the end of the 1946 season, and it was rumored that Frisch was on his way out, Ward stopped in at the Flash's suite in Pittsburgh's Schenley Hotel to find him reading.

"My future occupation," said Frisch, flashing a smile, pointing to the cover of the book, a best seller then. The title read, aptly, *Yankee Storekeeper.*

By then, Frisch had made USO trips to the Aleutians, then Europe in World War II. Before the Army hurried the Flash and Friends out of the grim Battle of the Bulge in December, 1944—he was accompanied by Mel Ott, Bucky Walters, and Emil (Dutch) Leonard, ball players, and Roy Stockton, writer and coordinator—he provided the comic relief.

"That Dutchman," said Stockton, "not only told the funniest stories, but he did the craziest things. Wherever the Army would bivouac us with a family, Frank would slip out a little Army chow or even a hard roll for them. Oh, how he loved that Holland chocolate. But whenever a bomb fell, he'd be the first guy under the kitchen table, moaning, 'What 'n hell am I doing here when I could be home eating Ada's cooking?' "

To get into baseball uniform, and into the game's pension plan, which then was available only to players, coaches, and trainers active in September, 1946, Frisch joined his old club, the Giants, as a coach in 1949 under his old teammate, Leo Durocher. Branch Rickey had told Durocher in 1937 that Frisch, with whom the Cardinals' captain thought he had a warm relationship, had issued a him-or-me ultimatum that led to Leo's move to Brooklyn, where in 1939 he succeeded Burleigh Grimes as manager. If Frisch did indeed put it the way Rickey said he did, Durocher was the bigger man for having agreed with owner Horace Stoneham to have Frisch as a Giants' coach.

The job lasted only temporarily, however, because, with Stoneham's permission, Charley Grimm approached the Old Flash at Phil Wrigley's

Blood, Guts, and Cripes: *When Frank Frisch was caught in the Battle of the Bulge entertaining American troops, he was properly scared. Here, before the Flash and pitcher Bucky Walters (next to him) were almost caught off base by the enemy, they met two top United States military leaders, Gens. Omar Bradley and George S. Patton.*

request in mid-season, 1949. One Dutchman had recommended the other as a managerial successor. Grimm admired Frisch's competitiveness.

The job, which paid $37,000, highest of Frisch's career, lasted almost exactly two seasons of poor, frustrating baseball. Except, that is, when on the final weekend of the 1949 season, the last-place Cubs rose up to take two out of three from the Cardinals, virtually guaranteeing Rickey's Brooklyn Dodgers the pennant St. Louis had seemed to have locked up.

The night before the season ended at Wrigley Field, Leo Ward and friends sat in the Redbird traveling secretary's suite for a wake that had been figured to be a pennant-clinching party. Suddenly, the suite doorbell rang, the door opened, and a hat came sailing into the room, followed by Frisch, who stayed at the same hotel, Chicago's Knickerbocker.

"I guess I'm not welcome here?" Frisch said, feigning timidity.

Ward growled an obscenity of lefthanded welcome, which was what Frisch was expecting.

"Crissake," he said, "don't blame me that your bustards couldn't beat my humpty-dumpties. Why, I'm over fifty years old, and I could hit that [Bob] Chipman with my eyes closed. Slid-uh—God, that's nothing except an old nickel curve. I could hit that with my bare ahm."

Everybody laughed. But the woeful Cubs weren't funny enough, or often enough, for Frisch, as recalled by big Bob Scheffing, former Chicago catcher, later manager of the Cubbies and Detroit Tigers, and general manager of the pennant-winning New York Mets.

"Frisch was a character, all right, good and funny, unintentionally funny as often as sarcastic. Grimm had played against him so long he felt the Flash's winning spirit would rub off, but Frank just couldn't tolerate or even understand mediocrity.

"One day, for instance, he made a late-inning, two-player position change, and put Wayne Terwilliger, a second baseman, at third base, and Bob Ramazotti, ordinarily a third baseman, at second. He gave me the lineup change to give the umpires, and I noticed the switch, and mentioned it to him.

"Frisch brushed it off. 'Hell,' he said, 'if you play second, third is child's play.'

"For a Frisch, maybe, but not for all. The first batter bunted one toward third, and Terwilliger threw it away. And the next one hit to Ramazotti, who kicked it.

"Frank had a puzzled look when I came to the bench afterward. He said, 'Cripes, you're right, Scheff. Some of these guys are cigar-store Indians out of position.'"

So Frisch went back to New York, unemployed, but not for long. He was doing color commentary before and after Giants' home games when he suffered a heart attack in 1956. He gave up smoking, but he never could rid himself of a taste for the rich-food or lose his sweet-tooth.

A hairshirt to the player then, and later, he'd label spring training of the latter day as "a country club without dues," and he decried the use of batting helmets.

Now Listen Here, Rob-ut:
In his best Bronx accent,
Frank Frisch came to
town to tell an audience
funny stories and to ex-
plain that he hadn't been
as good a manager when
he no longer could lead his
troops as a player.

**Oh, How Did I Get Into
This?:** Frank Frisch's de-
pressed look tells how
l-o-n-g and miserable life
was when he managed the
troubled Chicago Cubs,
1949-51.

"In my day," he maintained, "guys like [Burleigh] Grimes and [Dizzy] Dean would play tunes on those plastic thingamajigs, and make 'em sound like Swiss bell-ringers."

Many a player grumbled profanely about the old so-and-so, but it was typically Frisch, not knowing the difference between humor and sarcasm—or not caring. Still, he named two Cardinals in his aviary "Musial" and "Slaughter." He was close to Red Schoendienst, Lou Brock and to Stan Musial. Musial had traveled to the Aleutians with him during World War II and to Europe afterward.

Said, Frisch, "Every time Charley [Grimm] and I would find a new place for a little schnapps and fine German music or a chance to try out our low Dutch, I'd look up, and there would be Stanislaus and Jerry Coleman [Yankee infielder] peeking in to follow us. Still, I have to hand it to Musial. He learned how to play a zither from an old Bavarian."

By now, Frisch had begun to refer to himself more and more as the "Old Flash." He mellowed, delighting in telling how kids in New Rochelle would mimic his shrill moaning about son-of-a-witch walks. As they bicycled by as he was going out his door for a paper, watering his lawn or just sitting outside reading, they imitated his radio-tv lament.

"Hey, Flash," they'd yell to the grinning old timer, " 'Oh, those bases on balls.' "

In 1957, thirty years after he'd been put on the spot marked "X" by the trade that sent him to St. Louis from New York for Rogers Hornsby, Frisch came back for a speaking engagement. By then, he also teamed with professional writers for first-person magazine pieces under his by-line, and he botched a book with Stockton, an old pro who wasn't satisfied with their collaboration. Frisch wrote his own amusingly sarcastic speeches. Ada typed them, and he delivered his lines with timing and exquisite intonation.

Back there in '57 that full generation after the turning point in his colorful career took him from his own backyard to the new challenge of St. Louis, Frisch summed himself up in honest self-analysis.

"I was a better manager with a good ball club than with a bad one," he said. "I always wanted to win, and couldn't stand bad baseball. Those Cubs nearly killed me. Seems to me I put on the squeeze play seven times before one of my guys even fouled a ball. I guess I should have given him a box of cigars?"

See the good-natured sarcasm? Smiling, the Old Flash then summed himself up better than even his warmest friend or severest critic could.

"I think managing shortened my playing career, but I was a better manager when I was playing, when I could lead like a platoon sergeant in the field rather than as a general sitting back on his duff in a command post.

"But," he emphasized, the introspection turning to self-defense, "I won't apologize for having wanted my players to be as good as I was supposed to be. If intolerance of mediocrity is a crime, I plead guilty."

A Warrior in Repose: Frank Frisch, past 70, sits in his favorite chair near the Rhode Island seashore to read, surrounded by his two pet spaniels (1967).

Temporarily, just temporarily, he'd given up drinking. But arthritis or not, he couldn't resist wrapping himself around a double-dipped chocolate sundae laden with nuts and whipped cream. Sweet tooth, thy name was Flash.

"Flash," by the by, was his name for one of his English springer spaniels, "Patch" was the other. He'd sit with them by the seashore and read at Quonochontaug, Rhode Island, a tongue-twisting Indian name for "Big Black Fish." The Frischs had moved to a five-acre place there temporarily after his heart-attack recovery, but they'd fallen in love with the 450-population place, and moved to ebbtide the mementoes and memories of Frisch's career.

Scrawling marginal comments as he read, al fresco, the Old Flash wore a Redbird windbreaker and a Detroit Tigers' cap. Incongruous, sure, but wasn't Frank Frisch an incongruity, a cultured roughneck? The cap had come from pianist Istomin by way of Tigers' general manager Jimmy Campbell.

Now and then, Frisch would run up to Boston with friend Frank Sammataro, a Westerly, Rhode Island, real estate man, to watch the Red Sox at Fenway Park. Naturally, he made good use of televised baseball, too. As a proud member of the Baseball Hall of Fame, he loved the delightful village of Cooperstown, and the old-fashioned opulence of the Ot-e-sa-ga Hotel on the lakefront.

As a member of the Hall of Fame's Veterans' Committee, he could show old-timers' sentiment for his contemporaries, but he was also pragmatic enough to stump, for instance, for three shortstops who played their careers after he'd put aside that peewee glove, that educated bat and those ballet-sized baseball shoes.

"You don't win without great shortstops, no matter how much or how little they hit," said Frisch, mentioning Marty Marion, Phil Rizzuto, and Pee Wee Reese. If he had only seen switcher Garry Templeton, a dusky young Frisch . . .

Dear Ada died early in 1971, and Frisch, staggered, took all of his and her brothers, sisters, nieces, nephews, grand-nieces, and grand-nephews to Cooperstown for an expensive blowout at the annual Hall of Fame ceremonies that August.

In the summer of 1972, he married attractive Augusta Kass, and put on his figurative dancing slippers at Cooperstown with the younger, vivacious woman who played golf and taught handicapped children.

Frank Francis Frisch, gambling niggardly on old tires when his common sense told him he needed new ones, was driving from Florida to Rhode Island in February, 1973, when a tire blew, and he had an accident in which he was critically injured. Even so, the Old Flash lingered five weeks in a hospital and looked as if he had just beaten the game of life with a three-run double. Then he died of a heart attack on March 11.

Nearly forty years before, February, 1933, the year the man who became pilot light of the Gas House Gang lit the lamp as field foreman, an amateur palmist named O. E. Laroge of St. Louis sent *The Sporting News* a diagrammed reading on the super-star second baseman with the deformed middle finger on his right hand.

The palmist's analysis was sound. It said that Frisch "dislikes noise and fuss, is fond of travel, home, and has a rare combination of intuition and intellectual foresight. It is a hand of much self-confidence, and good leadership. His good nature makes many friends. He is cultured, self-sacrificing, and full of sympathy.

"He must overcome a sudden setback or accident, but he will live to a ripe old age; about seventy-five years."

When that motor mishap slipped a third strike past the Dutchman, Frankie Frisch was seventy-five years old.

A Funny Friend: *Casey Stengel, shown at the left as the Giants' outfielder, and then as Yankees' manager, was close to Frisch at the ball park, as well as the nearest bar.*

18
Casey and the Umps

So THE girth was gone, but the mirth lingers on, memories of Frankie Frisch, fiery and funny, competitor and comedian, gracious winner and hard loser. Most of the humor stems from his relationship with the men in blue, and an old teammate who was as colorful as the orange-tinted hair he favored late in his incredible octogenarian life.

Casey Stengel, who could outdrink, and outfox the Flash, could even out talk him. Not many umpires could say the same.

If there was one whose vocal chords were more lively, and even more shrill than Frisch's, it was John (Beans) Reardon, transplanted New England Yankee who found warmth, and prosperity at Long Beach, California, as distributor for Anheuser-Busch. That would be poetic justice, indeed, because as Gussie Busch would concede with a grin, even before the brewery bought the Cardinal ball club in 1953, Reardon consumed Budweiser as if he were . . . well, would you believe, Stengel or Frisch?

167

Actually, Stengel would drink just about anything alcoholic, and consume it in sizable gulps between sentences that were unpunctuated, with fractured syntax, not just broken. Most sentences, like broken bones, can be reset, but there was no way to recast the double-talk that became famous as Stengelese.

Few reporters, even those proud enough to say they'd been around the craggy-faced old cuss long enough to understand his oblique references, and version for common nouns—and I was "amongst 'em," as Dizzy Dean would say—could translate Stengelese with the accurate ear of a Red Smith, a John Carmichael or Frank Graham.

But in talking about old teammate Frisch, managerial rival and nightfall partner in small talk and large drinks, Stengel might ramble.

"I hafta say Mr. Frisch, which helps me play center field at the Polo Grounds where the fence was so far back I never could figure how Mr. McGraw could see into the clubhouse window from the dugout, was the first infielder who didn't do this . . . "

Here, Stengel would leap up from the bar stool and backpedal like a prize-fighter, simulating a ball player going back on a pop fly.

"Now, this feller [Frisch]," Stengel would continue in his rasping bourbon-enriched bass, demonstrating further by turning nearly 360 degrees, and running head down, arms pumping, "would go out with his back to the ball, racing at full speed, and turn just in time to catch the kind which I'd never seen anyone else do before, and he'd run so fast to the foul line at the close right field fence that he'd catch 'em before they could hit the right field wall, and you could look it up . . . . "

Stengel, eight years older than Frisch, played only two and one half seasons with the young Flash, but their comradeship blossomed when both became managers. Ol' Case was promoted from coach to manager in 1934, the year Frisch's Gas House Gang won the pennant in the last two days with considerable help from Stengel's Dodgers.

When the fifty-five-year-old Stengel's ball club knocked Bill Terry's team out of the running, that year in which Terry facetiously wondered whether Brooklyn was still in the National League, the opposing managers encountered each other outside the clubhouses some time after the last game.

Growled the bigger, younger Terry, "If your ball club had played all season the way you did the last two days, you wouldn't have finished sixth."

Rasped Stengel, "No, and if your fellers had-a played all season the way you did the last two, you wouldn't-a finished second."

Menacingly, Terry took a step toward Stengel, then turned on his heel, stalked off, hopped into a cab, and was gone from 155th Street to lick his wounds elsewhere.

Stengel would recall, "He could-a cleaned my clock, but I hafta say I'd-a got a piece of him, too."

Years later, reminded of that close encounter of the unpleasant kind, Casey was embarrassed. He would change the subject, and say, invariably, "But he [Terry] was really all right as well as a great ball player. At the winter meetings, we met in a hotel elevator, and he was very nice, which was very nice . . . "

The closest Stengel came to unhappiness with Frisch was after their last hurrah at a time the Old Flash was long since out of baseball. Ol' Case, a character of prominence after winning eleven pennants, and a record five straight world championships with the New York Yankees, was managing the miserable, misfit team he so often called "the Amazin' Mets." That adjective stuck, which you couldn't say about fly balls the Amazin's tried to catch.

Just a couple of years earlier at a 100th anniversary professional baseball celebration, to which the Cardinals invited all living members of the baseball Hall of Fame, there had been a party at Stan Musial's restaurant that got late, and l-a-t-e-r. Wetter, too, inside.

Frisch and Stengel were dancing the night away with young, attractive wives of Redbird club officials, and others present. Frisch had found an amused partner in lovely Jane Claiborne, wife of the young assistant who would succeed Bing Devine as the Cardinals' general manager. Suddenly, Uncle Frank felt a volcano erupting.

Excusing himself, he waddled into a men's room; and in quick order threw up, cleaned up, and popped a nitro glycerin pill into his mouth for the old heart. Sighing with a smile, he said, "Ah, yes, I can see the Old Flash helping make Musial more famous, and more money. The newspaper headlines will say, 'Frisch Succumbs in Musial's Toilet.' "

WHEN DAWN was coming up over Busch Memorial Stadium that summer morning in 1969, Frisch, Stengel, and host Musial carried another Hall of Famer into a riverfront hotel.

And it was coming up daylight at Toots Shor's oasis in New York another morning when Stengel wobbled into one cab and Frisch into another. Unfortunately, Ol' Case fell at his apartment, broke his hip, and was forced to give up as bench boss at Shea Stadium.

In an emergency basis at the hospital, they were forced to put Stengel in the maternity ward. Frisch promptly sent him roses and a bag of diaper pins.

The wrinkled, chalky old face would light up with the good joke when Frisch was gone. And he was still holding forth almost as when he'd drink "my writers" and coaches under a table, and then be up bright and early for breakfast.

"Trouble with that Frisch," complained the pot calling the kettle unpolished, "he didn't know when to go to bed."

Charles Dillon Stengel was unusual from the time he came out of Kansas City as a lefthanded dental student who went to Kankakee, Illinois, as an outfield candidate.

At Kankakee, the ball park was near the state mental institution, where the inmates took a shine to the silly center fielder they invited to come inside for the fun. When a game ended and the inmates cheered, their Casey, his nickname a short version of "Kay Cee," his home town, would sling his glove toward the fence, rush over toward it, and practice a fallaway slide.

"Good for my thowin'" he'd say because, to Stengel, he could never crowd an "r" into "throwing," and "also my runnin' and slidin' and enjoyable for those unfortunate creatures."

At Brooklyn, where he played from 1912 through the pennant-winning season of 1916, he was a favorite. When he came back in an enemy uniform, and was given a lusty Flatbush boo, he removed his cap in a sweeping bow. And, out flew another unfortunate creature he'd found in the outfield, an injured sparrow. The fans loved it.

Years later, when Mickey Mantle joined the Yankees, highly publicized as a blond Paul Bunyan of baseball, Stengel took Joe DiMaggio's rookie outfield partner to show him the tricky carom off the sloping right field fence at Brooklyn's Ebbets Field. Wide-eyed Mantle asked innocently, "Did YOU play here, Casey?"

Stengel grumbled, "Crissake, do you think I was born sixty-five years old?"

When he finished a fourteen-year career as a lefthanded hitter who batted .393 in three World Series, he was named playing manager and president at the Boston Braves' Worcester, Massachusetts, farm club of the Eastern League in 1925. He "did good, and you could look it up," as Stengel would say, and he was offered the job as player-manager at Toledo, Ohio, of the American Association in 1926.

Without consulting Boston, club president Stengel immediately released manager-player by letter, puckishly added a congratulatory comment. The Braves didn't see the humor of the situation at all.

Early Encounters: *Casey Stengel, manager at Boston, and Frank Frisch, Pittsburgh pilot, trying to hold back a laugh in 1942.*

But the clown, once paid a full year's salary NOT to manage (Brooklyn, 1937), became baseball's best ambassador. Not, however, before he and Frisch began their home-and-home series of nights out, in which they alternated in check-grabbing, stiffing each other with a tab, or finding their wit and charm in getting themselves invited from topflight hotel tables-for-two to wedding parties, and other enjoyable celebrations.

Routinely, after a game, whether in St. Louis, Boston, or Pittsburgh, the winner would phone the loser. Frisch was the most persistent, even if he had to phone from the lobby of Boston's Myles Standish, or wherever Ol' Case was staying. Or, as he did at least once, pound on the door to get his friend to open up sourly so that he could hit the town.

Once in 1934, when every game was important to the Cardinals, Frisch lost a tough one to Stengel's lowly Dodgers. Steaming, the Flash didn't even grab a cab with Mike Gonzalez to the Coronado Hotel, where he lived.

Instead, the hot-under-the-collar Flash walked the zig-zag course back toward the hotel. Stengel, who had missed him in the clubhouse, followed by cab and urged him to hop in. Frisch told him no, politely, and then not so politely. Casey persisted. He had the cab circle so that he could taunt or tease, but mainly tempt, coaxing with the charm of a male Circe.

Finally, persuasion won. Frisch surrendered with profanity, joined the grinning Stengel in the cab and drowned his sorrows that evening while Casey celebrated the rare pleasure of beating Frank's Redbirds.

The Jack Benny-Fred Allen "feud" couldn't have been funnier than Frisch and Stengel. In 1943, when Casey had a horrible team at Boston and the Flash a decent one at Pittsburgh, a taxicab felled Casey on a rainy night at Kenmore Square.

Frisch sent a sympathetic telegram to the hospital.

"YOUR ATTEMPT AT SUICIDE FULLY UNDERSTOOD. DEEPEST SYMPATHY YOU DIDN'T SUCCEED."

Stengel reciprocated often, including the time an apparent game-winning, two-run homer by Pittsburgh's Jim Russell had been nullified because Pirate infielder Frankie Zak, on base, had just called time to tie a shoe lace.

Stengel wired gleefully, "AM RUSHING PAIR OF BUTTON SHOES FOR ZAK."

When Frisch's old spike wound acted up at Pittsburgh, and the Flash sat in uniform at Boston with one foot, carpet-slippered, propped up gingerly in his dugout, Stengel came by, clucked compassionately. Then when Frankie was lulled into complacency, Casey snarled:

"That ain't a foot, you old fraud. That's a claw left over from all those lobsters you ate that year you were on radio here."

Stengel left the Old Flash sputtering, just as he did another time. Frisch was bedded down at Pittsburgh's Schenley Hotel, immobilized after surgery on the long-troublesome foot. From the late, lamented

Schenley's excellent cuisine, Frisch had ordered room service. The food came just as Stengel arrived in the suite. Casey's eyes lighted up like a pinball machine on tilt.

"Put it right over here, young man," he directed. And while Frisch protested, alternately begging for his dinner and cussing, Ol' Case consumed the Old Flash's steak dinner with a running, mouth-watering, gourmet play-by-play.

Once, Stengel even caught Frisch in a batting-order boo-boo. Intending to play Stu Martin at second base to lead off for the Pirates, Frisch had told Frank Gustine he was playing.

In Pittsburgh's home half, after Gustine opened with a single, Stengel trotted out to plate umpire Jocko Conlan, and said, pointing to the runner, "Do you see what I see?"

Conlan did. "Yeah," he said, "Gustine, you're out."

Angry at himself, Frisch tore up his batting-order cards. But, the umpire had booted one, too. Gustine was not out for having batted out of turn. He was merely an unannounced substitute and should have been permitted to stay on base, Frisch merely subjected to a rule-book $25 fine. Furthermore, because Pittsburgh scored a run in that first inning even after Gustine had been declared out unfairly, a Pirate protest of a game lost only 3-1 probably would have been upheld.

Stengel's pleasure was doubled, just as Frisch's had been at Mr. Wrigley's field back in 1934, when he caught old umpiring antagonist Bill Klem in a misinterpretation of a rule.

With a powerful wind in the Windy City blowing out to left field, the Cubs, leading handsomely in the late innings behind Lon Warneke, had the bases loaded with one out when Chuck Klein lofted a high foul "up the elevator shaft," as they say on the diamond. Catcher Bill DeLancey turned, facing the stands, then backpedaled awkwardly, too late, as the ball fell untouched, fair.

A run scored, and Klein reached base before Frisch, accompanied by his captain, Durocher, raised Hail, Columbia with Klem, claiming application of the infield-fly rule under which, except on a line drive, a batter is automatically out with fewer than two out, and first and second, or all three, bases occupied. That is, on a fly ball "that can be handled by an infielder."

One apocryphal version is that Klem, in his stentorian tones, roared, "Since when is a catcher an infielder?"

John Heydler, retiring that year as National League president, upheld the protest and ordered the game resumed. But the Cards won only on paper, not the field.

Where and when Frank Francis Frisch became an umpire baiter is difficult to determine, but it's evident that even as a player concentrating keenly on winning, he delighted in sparring orally with the men in blue. Such as when he was a younger super-star who traveled swiftly. Now and again, he would dive spectacularly into first base in an attempt to beat out a bunt dragged toward first or pushed toward third, or on a grounder chopped high or slowly to an infielder.

A National League umpire who had been a football coach when Centre College's Praying Colonels upset Harvard in 1921, 6-0, was bow-tied Charley Moran. Moran had a habit of grasping his coat lapels when working the bases, and casually flipping a thumb in an "out" motion without wasted effort.

One day, Frisch, trying so-o-o hard, flung himself head-first into first base on a bang-bang play. But Moran, determining the Flash's bust-a-gut effort was just too late, boringly jerked the coat-grasping thumb in a sign that deprived Frisch of a basehit, the Cardinals of a scoring opportunity.

The Flash leaped to his feet, not to question the umpire's judgment, but his technique.

"Dammit, Uncle Charley," he began.

"Don't call me 'Uncle Charley,'" interrupted the umpire, who didn't like to be Uncle-Charleyed.

"Dammit, Uncle Charley," Frisch repeated, "I bust my butt trying to beat a close play, and you give me that half-assed 'out' signal. Criminy, can't you do better than that?"

Later, smiling, Frisch recalled that the next time he grounded out, he was out by plenty. But as he stepped on first base, and turned to head for his dugout, Moran removed his hand from the coat lapel. Reaching back like a pitcher bringing up smoke from the ground, he followed through 180 degrees to the other side of the bag, roaring.

"You're O-U-T, young man, and is that enough effort and enthusiasm for you?"

"Fine, Uncle Charley," Frisch said, "fine."

Frisch would stick his crooked nose in an umpire's face and cackle like a galded gander, but he never really engaged in any physical contact, unlike his first lieutenant, Durocher, who wound up, years later, as a Dodger coach at Los Angeles in a shin-kicking contest with Jocko Conlan.

"I lost that one," said Durocher, "because Jock was wearing his steel-tipped plate umpire's shoes."

Frisch could use some of the nastiest language. Cutting comments would "win" him the rest of the day off and cost him enough $50 and $100 fines to help pay the umpires' pensions. But he was entirely taken aback in 1934 in a game against the Cubs at St. Louis. Joe Medwick, sliding hard, appeared to score the winning run on an extra-base hit by Durocher, and even Gabby Hartnett, catching for Chicago, started off the field.

But, Cy Rigler astonished the Cardinals and a crushed crowd by declaring Medwick "out", bringing Frisch storming off the third-base bench at Sportsman's Park so fast that he apparently skidded into the umpire, who, carrying his mask, immediately thumped Frisch on the side of the head with the iron-and-wire face protector.

Stunned more in surprise than in injury, the Old Flash stammered, "Why . . . Cy . . . Cy . . . "

Rigler was fined. So was Frisch, but Frank felt sorrier for the umpire. After all, they were getting no virgin when they stuck him for a few bucks or more. There were no hard feelings, though, because he was Heydler's favorite. And the retiring league president labeled the Dutchman's 1934 Series double as his pet play of Heydler's final World Series as president.

Frisch was a favorite of the former sportswriter and radio man, Ford Frick, the league president who became commissioner. What Frick and the umpires liked about Frisch was that he carried no grudges, which some arbiters felt Durocher did. The Flash would fight like blazes for today's game, but tomorrow's was a different one. His disgust with a losing cause did seem to bring out the best in his humor.

For instance, he once phoned Frick at New York from Pittsburgh and talked of many things, not only the notice of financial assessment he'd received. Suddenly the league president smelled a rat.

"Hey," Frick said, "I accepted this as a collect call. You're trying to get your fine back at the league's expense. Goodbye."

Another time a little bird whispered to the league president that Frisch planned to pay a $100 fine by trundling a large sack of pennies out to home plate. Frisch got the point in Frick's pointed telegram, "DON'T, DUTCHMAN."

Those inferior ball clubs brought out the superior side in the old ham. The portly pixie was thrown out of one game for going out to home plate carrying an umbrella, a suggestion, too slapstick, that Jupiter Pluvius should be carrying the day. He was also photographed giving a mocking, sweeping bow to glaring George Magerkurth after big Maje had cleared Frisch's bench at Pittsburgh.

Maybe, having fun was Frank's way to keep from crying as the former perfectionist was plagued by incompetence. One day, he was coaching third base for the Pirates at Chicago when Zak, his light-hitting shortstop, tried to score from first on an apparent triple by Jim Russell. As Zak rounded third, he was hipped off the baseline by sly Eddie Stanky, the Chicago third baseman, and almost catapulted into the third-base dugout.

Frisch had seen the McGravian muggerism, which infuriated him. But so had the umpire, Conlan, who immediately shouted, "Obstruction! Runner scores."

Frisch, excited and unsatisfied, waited until Russell rushed around to third base. As the runner slid in from the second-base approach, the Flash hook-slid into the bag from the coach's box. Stanky tagged Frisch, and missed Russell.

Conlan snapped, pointing to Russell, "He's safe," and then, pointing to Frisch, "and you're out—outta the game."

Frisch, as Bill Klem's pet, delighted Klem because he had been such a National League blue-chip performer in World Series and All-Star play.

Frank could get by with more in their salty exchanges than other players or managers. He wasn't foolish enough to call Klem by the nickname he detested, "Catfish," so appropriate because the wide-mouthed ump looked like a gaping-capped fish. But when Klem would draw his famous end-of-comment physical line, Frisch would take the care to circumvent it. He'd walk, not over, but AROUND it. Once, he had Klem box himself in with four lines before pointing down at the square and walking away chortling.

Good things can be overdone, though. At Pittsburgh one afternoon, Frank feigned a faint at an adverse call, stiffening in the coach's box, and keeling over backward.

As Pittsburgh players rushed out, Klem came up the baseline, closed one eye like Wallace Beery in a movie, and roared, "If you ain't dead, Frisch, you're out of the game."

Whether cheek to jowl in argument on the field or in drinking bouts, listening to Max Steindel of the St. Louis symphony pick out on a cello at the Coronado Hotel, the kind of music the incongruous, rough-and-refined Frisch liked, the Flash's favorite companion among arbiters was Beans Reardon.

It was Reardon who caught on to the Flash's favorite hot-weather device in New York, where he loved to stay at his restful suburban home in New Rochelle or, at least, get a head start before the late-afternoon traffic. With Ada, he could tend fondly to his roses, rhododendron, laurel, azalea, yew and American holly. How could a guy compare fifty bucks with a peaceful day in the garden or on the veranda?

One particularly hot day at the Polo Grounds, Frisch went to work early on Reardon, but Beans, who ordinarily swapped insults and vulgarities with him, was silent. Finally, the umpire beckoned him to home plate.

"Listen, Hap,"—Reardon called Frisch "Happy" because the ump thought Frank was always moaning about his health when he wasn't groaning about his players—"I'm staying out here for all nine [innings] today, and so are you. So, save your breath, or Ada's husband may get a stroke."

Frisch, giving Reardon a going-over from the bench one game, suddenly mumbled something. The umpire whipped off his mask wheeled toward Frank's bench.

"What did you say?" he asked, hotly.

Sweetly, Frisch replied, "You've been guessing all day. Now, guess what I said?"

The smart-aleck comment got the Flash the rest of the afternoon to contemplate his belly button, or whatever.

Not all ejections brought fines, but umpires were required to wire precisely what was said to them to the office. Many a Western Union girl's ears must have curled from some of the comments and counter-comments. Reardon would not lie about getting his own few dollars' worth into a bitter exchange.

Still, business was business, fun was monkey business. Reardon could throw Frisch out of a game in St. Louis, join him and Mike Gonzalez for a beer or two at the hotel afterward, and then borrow the Old Flash's new Packard. From the hotel garage, the phone would ring, and Reardon's voice would rasp, "Hey, Hap, tell this joker to fill the gas tank."

Years later, Reardon would cackle, "And the next day the Flash gave me too much lip, and I threw him out of the game again, and recommended a fine. What a guy! There never was another like him!"

An original Dutch master, all right, the brilliant ball player once walked out of a meeting at Ford Frick's office when he came in for a hearing just in time to hear that an umpire's job might be at stake. "Good day, gentlemen," said Frankie, putting on his hat, "no call, no matter how lousy, is worth the firing of an umpire."

Frisch received what was probably his finest athletic compliment from Joe McCarthy, the great Cub-Yankee manager who lived to a ripe old ninety. Marse Joe, a man of few words, was asked one day by a magazine writer to give him a composite perfect player.

"A what?" inquired McCarthy.

"Oh, you know what I mean," said the writer, "what you would take in every department? Would it be Cobb or Ruth hitting or someone who fielded like DiMaggio, or ran like . . . "

Quietly, McCarthy interrupted him. "What are you going to all that trouble for?" said the famous manager. "What couldn't Frank Frisch do?"

Well, for one thing, he probably couldn't handle men or manage as well as McCarthy, but he did have an amusing formula for field foremen that he passed along to a young friend, Red Schoendienst, when another St. Louis second-base successor became manager of the Cardinals. Said Frisch, with that devilish grin, as the heavy-lidded brown beagle eyes squinted, "Just stay away from firearms, Red, and don't room higher than the second floor. You might want to jump."

Years earlier, after he had struck one blow for managerial brilliance with that base-clearing double that broke up the 1934 World Series, the Old Flash struck one for all managers—past, present and future.

Coaching third base at Pittsburgh's Forbes Field, he listened patiently as a heckling boxseat occupant second-guessed him loudly. As he went back and forth to the bench, wearing a disarming smile, the manager began to solicit suggestions. What would the patron prefer? The pleased customer asked for a bunt here, a hit-and-run there, and . . .

Politely, at last, the Old Flash asked the fan's name, and where he worked. The man beamed, turning to his companions with a how-about-that-look, and gave name, rank, serial number and downtown address. But why would the Old Flash want to know?

"Because," blazed fire-eating Frank Frisch, the funny Fordham Flash, "I'm going to be down at your office tomorrow morning, flannelmouth, and tell you how to run your blankety-blank business."